Beginning Mental Tr

Skills for Badminton

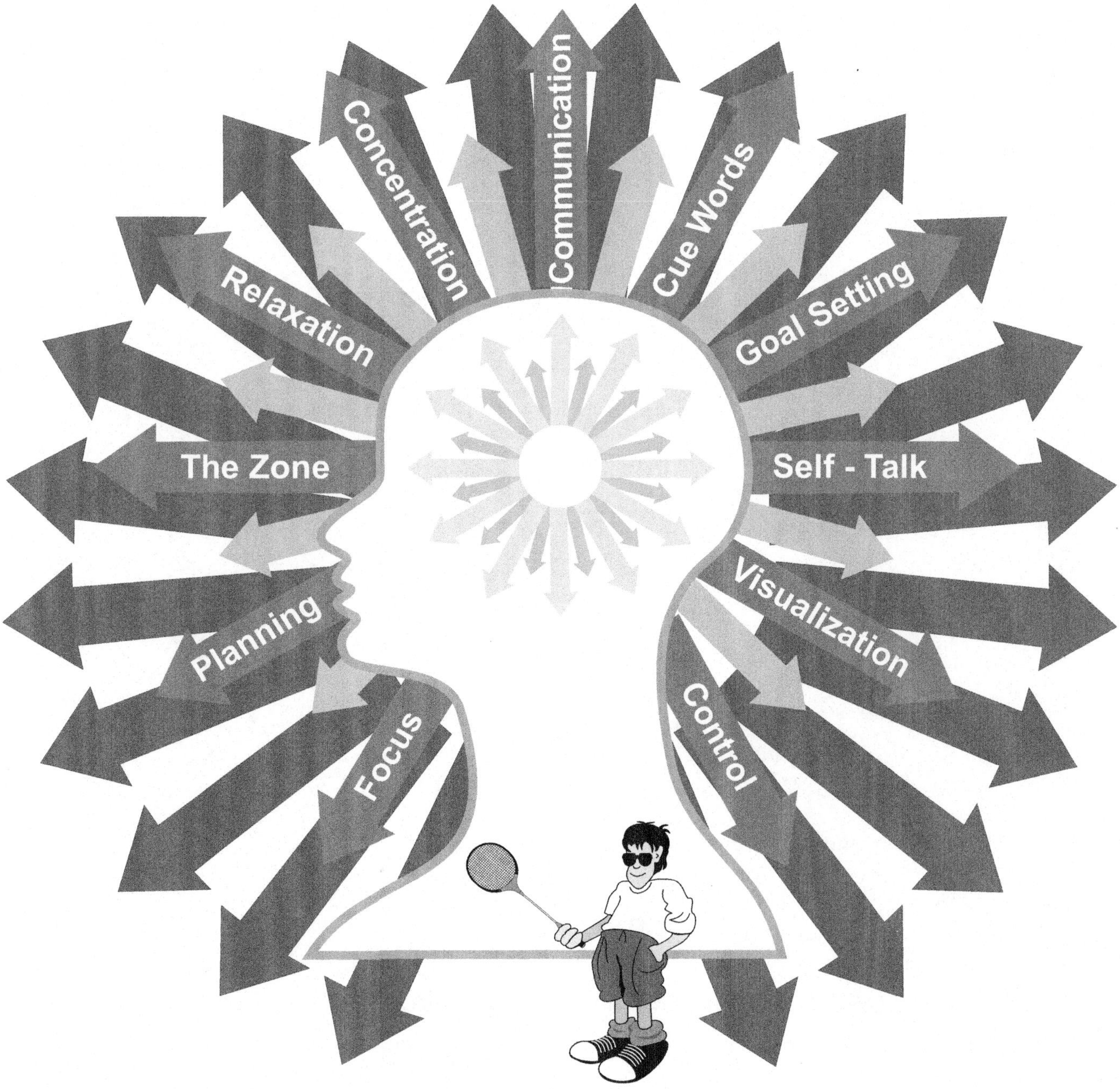

©2015 by Standup Productions
ISBN 9781516826797
Re-Published 2012
Charleston, SC
email: info@shannonmcdougall.com

webpage: http://www.beginningmentaltrainingskills.com

Table of Contents

Notes:

Preface

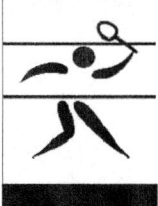

Beginning a mental training program can be intimidating and difficult without direction. This educational workbook is meant to give you an introduction to one of the most useful tools in sport. Mental training is considered by most to be a critical ingredient to success, yet it is one of the last things to be included in training and competition. By using this tool you can take control of your mental training future and your future in badminton.

This tool contains activities that progressively build on each other so you will be capable of keeping a positive and productive mental state when you need to. All you need is 15 - 20 minutes a day to gain a good understanding of mental training skills and to feel that you are achieving success at whatever level you are competing at.

The best time to begin a mental training program is just after your season ends in preparation for your next season. It will give you familiarity with psychological skills as you begin your next competitive season and then help you to refine your skills for the important competitions. This doesn't mean that you won't benefit if you begin working through the workbook after your season has started. You will definitely be able to add to your skills and it will give you some familiarity with the concepts as you begin your next season.

Many have found it useful to use a new workbook for each season because you may want to make adjustments if your competitive environment changes. If you would like to work on a second workbook after you have completed this one, simply contact me and I'll send you a PDF of the workbook without the content.

Cheers.
Shannon McDougall
www.beginningmentaltrainingskills.com

Notes:

Goal Setting

Goals are what we strive toward. The most important thing to remember is that goals need to be relevant to your situation only. You need to consider what level you're playing at, and what you want to achieve. If you play recreational badminton once a week at the community centre, or competitive badminton in tournaments, mental training is just as important and can be just as beneficial to you regardless. Your goals are about you and your experience. Everyone is important and your goals should reflect your level of involvement, not the level you think you should be at.

How you achieve your goals is determined by the planning process and the steps that you take in that planning. Goals must be attainable, measurable, and must be evaluated so that you can make sure you are on the right track. Setting a time frame and check points will allow you to monitor your progress. If you find you are having difficulty at any of your check points, then you can re-evaluate the goal and make adjustments if you need to.

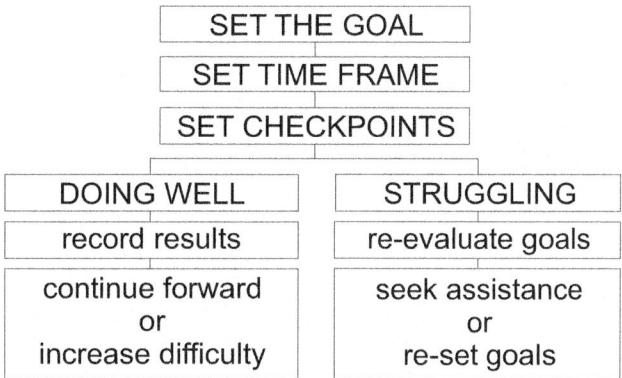

To set short term goals without achieving them is frustrating, and can prevent you from setting new goals. If your goals are out of reach, it will not only effect your ability to achieve the goals, but will also effect your confidence. Working hard toward a goal that is not achievable might seem endless and might even contribute to you leaving badminton, re evaluating your goals is will help you to prevent this.

The ability to measure your goals, is critical in monitoring your progress and making sure you are on the right track. This allows you to make changes if you need to by recording your progress. Set monitoring to happen just before the season begins, and watch through the season. and again after your season is done to reflect on your achievements. Use your record keeping to evaluate your goals for the next season.

Training Goals

Training goals, or practice goals are generally more directed towards physical and technical skills training. To increase your speed by 10% for example is a training goal that will help your technical performance in moving around the court. Knowing what kinds of physical skills benefit badminton and even what energy system is used will be important in setting your physical goals. Use your coach or athletic trainer as a resource if you are unsure and want to build your specific physical abilities.

Notes:

Goal Setting

Technical and tactical goals are the ones that enable you to play badminton. Most times they are established by your coach simply by the training sessions they schedule and the tasks that they schedule during the session. By working with your coach or a badminton instructor, you can find out where you need to improve and then set your goals accordingly.

Competition Goals

Competition is where all of your skills are put to the test. This is where anxiety and distractions are most likely to occur on a larger scale because you believe something is on the line. When you combine that with the difficulties that come with having low confidence and being afraid to perform poorly, this will become the focus instead of feeling the excitement of having fun and performing well. Goal setting for competition should refer to the execution of your badminton skills under stressful situations and maintaining your focus through distractions.

By having specific goals set for your game, it can help you to focus more on the process or just competing instead of worrying about the outcome of the match. The score, the importance of the match, and fear of failure can create self doubt and anxiety. Personal goals that are simple and focused on your performance process will help you to enjoy everything you love about badminton.

Goal Setting for Youth

Children need to have simple and easy yet challenging goals for their activities. It is also important for goals to be focussed on general skills that are not too complicated. The best way to set goals for children is to set achievable ones that make them feel good about themselves. Children need to feel like they are succeeding at something real and that they are doing things right. By giving them many opportunities to see themselves having success, they will begin building their overall sport confidence.

Making goals easy for youth to understand and evaluate, will help to develop their ability to process the steps needed for effective goal setting. Also, it is important to encourage their goal setting outside of badminton as well. This will benefit them as they are manoeuvring through school and other achievements.

Goal Setting for Adolescents

These athletes are often entering the specialization phase of badminton. Athletes younger than this should still be participating in multi sport activities thus their goals will be more multi skill oriented. As badminton specialization approaches, there will be more involvement from coaches and trainers in setting simple and attainable goals. For maximum effectiveness, their goals should continue to follow the principles of being simple, attainable and measurably.

Adolescents who are not necessarily specializing in badminton, can still use goal setting to help them to prevent anxiety during competition. They may choose to not use all of the goal setting activities and might only use the ones geared towards competition. The goals they set might relate to preparations, basic sports skills, and dealing with anxiety instead of specific physical and advanced technical or tactical goals.

Notes:

Goal Setting

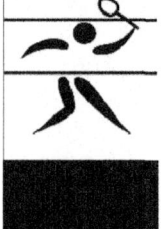

Goal Setting for Adults

You may be a new badminton player or someone who has played for a long time but just want to improve your competition experience. As a new player there are so many aspects of sport that can cause stress. Comparing yourself to others and self awareness are in my experience the two biggest obstacles when entering sport regardless of the which one you are in.

Setting goals that are related to your skill level will give you something to strive towards that is related to your personal skills rather than another player's skills. By allowing yourself to be a beginner and by setting achievable goals, you can enjoy true successes. This can be a hard task when you are so aware of your own abilities or inabilities.

Share with a close supporter what your goals are so they can help you to celebrate the small successes and stay focussed on your own performance.

The Exercises

I have broken the goal setting down into physical, technical and mental goals to allow you to break it down into smaller parts. Be as detailed as you can with the dream goals, pre-season goals and season goals so that you can focus on the most relevant things at the most relevant times.

Physical goals, are goals that you want to achieve that effect the physical part of badminton such as speed, flexibility and agility. This type of work is most times done in a gym or on the court and does not necessarily need your racquet to improve. If you are specializing in badminton and are at an advance level, you might need to use equipment.

Your Technical / Tactical goals are specific to badminton. For example you might want to be able to snap your wrist quickly on the return at the net. Or depending on the level that you play at, you might want to be able to serve to the exact spot at least 70% of the time for this season, and your dream goal might be to hit the target 100% of the time. This is where the attainability is important. If you strive to achieve something you are not yet capable of, you might be tempted to give up through frustration. Make sure the goals are as measurable as possible and they are achievable to guarantee success.

Mental or psychological goals are mostly related to your emotions and how they effect your performance. Did you know that as your anxiety level increases, your skill level can decrease substantially? The ability to compete with minimal psychological interference, will guarantee that you will not only perform better but you will enjoy the experience much more as well. You will find mental training skills that you learn in this book will be useful in your daily life as well. How good is that?

Dream Goal(s)

What would be the most perfect outcome that you would like to achieve? If you could achieve anything in badminton, what would it be? Write this down in your dream goals section. How do your physical, technical and mental skills need to be improved for you achieve your dream goal. Remember that this goal may take longer than a season depending on your current skill level and the path that you take to get there.

Notes:

Goal Setting

A dream goal is your ultimate goal in badminton. Something that maybe you might even think you can not achieve. That is the point of this goal. It is your DREAM goal. If you could do anything you want, what would it be? Allow yourself to dream because it will motivate you as you work through your pre-season and season goals.

It may be that you never fully achieve your dream goal. Yes this is in fact possible. However, this does not mean that you fail. It means that because you have a dream goal and something to strive towards, it will motivate you to be successful in your season goals.

Season Goals

Using your dream goals as a guide, what do you want to achieve during the season? Being able to break down your physical, mental and technical skills will make it easier to focus on one thing at a time without being overwhelmed by what is needed for your dream goals. You will be focussing on the details of the process for the season instead of the outcome of your dream goals. Make sure you to use the goal setting principles of having goals that are attainable, measurable and adjustable.

Pre-Season Goals

What is important in your preparations to have a successful season? This is the time to work on your physical skills, learn new technical/tactical skills and learn mental training skills. This is the preparation time where you look at your season goals and do what you can to give yourself the best opportunity to have success at those goals. Your pre-season goals are your path to what you will want to accomplish during your season.

Competition / Training Goals

Now is the time to break your goals down even further into specific, attainable and measurable goals for your practice or a specific competition. The goals for your training session or competition need to be achieved during that specific session. For example a goal for training might be to say only positive things to yourself after every play, It might be to make 80% of your executions perfect or to make sure you say at least one thing positive to your double's teamate during the session. Review these goals after the event and check off your successes.

Enjoy the Process

Playing sport is an amazing experience, and will bring every emotion from ecstatic excitement to down right anger. Much of this emotion is within your control. Choose to make your sport experience enjoyable, by taking steps to make sure you are not over extending yourself, or putting too many expectations on your performance. Pace your goals to meet success as you can.

Congratulate yourself regularly and you will always be looking forward to getting your gear together for the training session or match. You want to be a participant for life.

Notes:

Dream Goal(s)

5

ie: to win 70% of my games

Where I'm at now

Physical (what kind of physical shape am I in now?)

ie: I need to work on my hand eye coordination

Mental (how do I use psychological tools, do I understand them?)

ie: I need to be able to anticipate the opponents next move

Technical (what is my skill level now?)

ie: I need to improve my body control

What do I need to do?

Physical (what kind of workout should I pursue?)

ie: have a fitness instructor set up a program for me

Mental (what can I do to improve my use of psychological skills?)

ie: learn the game and how to observe opponents

Technical (how do I need to improve my skills?)

ie: practice hitting a shuttle into the air to get used to the distance that my racquet head should be from my body

Notes:

Physical Performance Plan 6

What do I need to work on? (be specific on weaknesses)

Strength
_____
ie: upper body strength

Speed
_____
ie: moving around the court

Flexibility
_____
ie: increase flexibility in my knees, hips and shoulders

Endurance
_____
ie: be able to play back to back games without getting tired

Agility
_____
ie: quick feet

How can I improve it? (what types of exercises/activities?)

Strength
_____
ie: bench press, military press, etc.

Speed
_____
ie: practice quickly moving around the court in all directions

Flexibility
_____
ie: specific exercise names

Endurance
_____
ie: running, stairmaster

Agility
_____
ie: shuffling exercises

How often do I need to work on it? (for best results)

Strength
_____
ie: 3-4 times per week

Speed
_____
ie: before practices

Flexibility
_____
ie: daily

Endurance
_____
ie: 1 hour 3 times per week

Agility
_____
ie: 3-4 times per week

Notes:

Mental Performance Plan ⑦

What do I need to work on? (be specific on weaknesses)

Relaxation _____
ie: staying calm in a big game

Preparation _____
ie: plans before the game

Focusing _____
ie: being aware of every move my opponent makes

Teamwork _____
ie: encouraging others

Visualization _____
ie: being able to use it during games

Self-Talk _____
ie: staying positive after errors

How can I improve it? (what types of exercises/activities?)

Relaxation _____
ie: breathing techniques

Preparation _____
ie: write out plans before games and practices

Focusing _____
ie: practice watching one player at a time, gradually watcing both players in a doubles match

Teamwork _____
ie: say at least one encouraging thing to someone during practices and games

Visualization _____
ie: practice short visualization exercises

Self-Talk _____
ie: use self-talk in daily life

How often do I need to work on it? (for best results)

Relaxation _____
ie: daily

Preparation _____
ie: before practices and games

Focusing _____
ie: at all practices and games

Teamwork _____
ie: at all practices and games

Visualization _____
ie: daily

Self-Talk _____
ie: daily

Notes:

Technical Performance Plan ⑧

What do I need to work on? (be specific on weaknesses)

Skill	What needs to be worked on
ie: forehand	ie: hitting the shuttle exactly where I want it to go consistently
ie: lob stroke	ie: getting the shuttle deep but not out
ie: serving	ie: the toss serve

How can I improve it? (what types of exercises/activities?)

Skill	How to improve it
ie: forehand	ie: practice hitting the shuttle in the air snapping the wrist at the point of contact
ie: lob stroke	ie: practice the overhead stroke contacting the shuttle away from my body
ie: serving	ie: practice cocking my wrist as the serve is made

How often do I need to work on it? (for best results)

Skill	When to work on it
ie: forehand	ie: minimum 3 times per week
ie: lob stroke	ie: minimum 3 times per week
ie: serving	ie: minimum 3 times per week

Notes:

Pre-Season Goal(s)

9

_____

_____

_____

Where I'm at now

Physical (what kind of physical shape am I in now?)

_____

Mental (how do I use psychological tools, do I understand them?)

_____

Technical (what is my skill level now?)

_____

What do I need to do?

Physical (what kind of workout should I pursue?)

_____

Mental (what can I do to improve my use of psychological skills?)

_____

Technical (how do I need to improve my skills?)

_____

Notes:

Physical Performance Plan

10

What do I need to work on? (be specific on weaknesses)

Strength _____

Speed _____

Flexibility _____

Endurance _____

Agility _____

How can I improve it? (what types of exercises/activities?)

Strength _____

Speed _____

Flexibility _____

Endurance _____

Agility _____

How often do I need to work on it? (for best results)

Strength _____

Speed _____

Flexibility _____

Endurance _____

Agility _____

Notes:

Mental Performance Plan   **11**

What do I need to work on? (be specific on weaknesses)

Relaxation _____

Preparation _____

Focusing _____

Teamwork _____

Visualization _____

Self-Talk _____

How can I improve it? (what types of exercises/activities?)

Relaxation _____

Preparation _____

Focusing _____

Teamwork _____

Visualization _____

Self-Talk _____

How often do I need to work on it? (for best results)

Relaxation _____

Preparation _____

Focusing _____

Teamwork _____

Visualization _____

Self-Talk _____

Notes:

Technical Performance Plan   12

What do I need to work on? (be specific on weaknesses)

Skill   What needs to be worked on

How can I improve it? (what types of exercises/activities?)

Skill   How to improve it

How often do I need to work on it? (for best results)

Skill   When to work on it

Notes:

Season Goal(s)

13

_____

_____

_____

Where I'm at now

Physical (what kind of physical shape am I in now?)

_____

Mental (how do I use psychological tools, do I understand them?)

_____

Technical (what is my skill level now?)

_____

What do I need to do?

Physical (what kind of workout should I pursue?)

_____

Mental (what can I do to improve my use of psychological skills?)

_____

Technical (how do I need to improve my skills?)

_____

Notes:

Physical Performance Plan

What do I need to work on? (be specific on weaknesses)

Strength _____

Speed _____

Flexibility _____

Endurance _____

Agility _____

How can I improve it? (what types of exercises/activities?)

Strength _____

Speed _____

Flexibility _____

Endurance _____

Agility _____

How often do I need to work on it? (for best results)

Strength _____

Speed _____

Flexibility _____

Endurance _____

Agility _____

Notes:

Mental Performance Plan

15

What do I need to work on? (be specific on weaknesses)

Relaxation _____

Preparation _____

Focusing _____

Teamwork _____

Visualization _____

Self-Talk _____

How can I improve it? (what types of exercises/activities?)

Relaxation _____

Preparation _____

Focusing _____

Teamwork _____

Visualization _____

Self-Talk _____

How often do I need to work on it? (for best results)

Relaxation _____

Preparation _____

Focusing _____

Teamwork _____

Visualization _____

Self-Talk _____

Notes:

Technical Performance Plan

What do I need to work on? (be specific on weaknesses)

Skill | What needs to be worked on

How can I improve it? (what types of exercises/activities?)

Skill | How to improve it

How often do I need to work on it? (for best results)

Skill | When to work on it

Notes:

Game/Practice Goals

(Photocopy for each game/practice) Write down your mental, physical or technical goals for the upcoming game/practice and how you are going to achieve them. After the game/practice, record how it went for you, did you achieve your goal, did you achieve part of your goal?

Goal(s):

Physical:

Mental:

Technical:

How am I going to achieve it (them)?:

Physical:

Mental:

Technical:

Results:

Physical:

Mental:

Technical:

Notes:

Communication

We communicate continually every day with ourselves and others and sometimes we do this every hour of the day while we are awake, weather we know it or not. The ability to consciously communicate a clear message without the possibility of miss interpretation takes a conscious effort and becomes easier with practice.

Following are some things that effect the way we communicate:

- the audience
- your relationship with the audience
- the desired outcome of the message
- two way communication

The Audience

Most of us communicate with everyone the same way, and believe that everyone understands what we are saying. You might find that communication with team mates or coaches is different than communicating with your best friend or your family. For example when you are wanting to get help from your coach with your skills, you will need to be specific in telling him/her what you need. Your communications will be more business like and with a goal in mind. If you are communicating with officials, you need to be professional and respectful of their position and importance in your competition. You might also communicate differently with your teammate, depending on the situation and the culture of your group.

Your Relationship with the Receiver

If you are new to a team, you may be more hesitant to be open and to speak freely until you feel more comfortable in the group. You may be nervous with the coach or not even talk to officials while you are finding your way through competitions and training, and getting to know everyone. You might be a player that has been with the team since you started and feel confident with everyone so you can speak more freely and feel more comfortable asking for assistance from your coach. Sometimes people are afraid of the reaction they might get from the receiver. Just be clear and open to questions so that you can make sure the right message is being heard and there is no room for misunderstanding.

Desired Outcome

Knowing what the message is that you are trying to get across is not always enough to make sure that the receiver is hearing and understanding what you are trying to say. By learning how to communicate using clear messages and by using non verbal communication, you can express your thoughts and be open to questions if they need clarification. It is important to allow questions and to be open to others opinions and viewpoints. At the end of a conversation, you may not agree with the recipient and that needs to be ok. Sometimes you just need to agree to disagree. You will however need to decide what you are going to do with that feeling if you need to. It all depends on the desired outcome and the importance of that outcome.

Notes:

Communication

Two Way Communication

The ability to listen and hear a message is critical to making sure that we are participating as effectively as we can within the conversation. Listening with an open mind will also contribute to your success in the exchange. Often people listen to someone, but as they are hearing what they are saying, they are formulating their response or making a judgement on what is being said before the sentence is finished. It is important to listen all the way through and even ask questions if you are not entirely sure of the message being given.

It is also easy when receiving a message to take things personally that are not meant to be personal. Be sure you are very informed of the intent of your conversations with others before making any judgements.

Use the communication section of the workbook to explore the different aspects of communication in your environment on and off the court. Observe others communication strategies and their effectiveness and then record your own thoughts.

Types of communication

There are three types of communication we use whether we are aware of it or not. They include:

1. *Verbal Communication:* The chosen use of words can be done either effectively or ineffectively. It is important to even rehearse what you are going to say if you need to discuss something that can be misinterpreted with someone. When verbally communicating in general, it is important still to be clear and open to questions and clarification from the receiver;

2. *Non-Verbal Communication:* People are always reading and reacting to each other in badminton. In the sports world, there are so many emotions that it is easy to read someone's body language louder than their words, and thus take things the wrong way. Someone could be angry about a play they made or believe an error was made, and you might think they are angry at you for something due to the way they brushed past you. It is important that, unless verbal communication was directed specifically at you along with the non-verbal communication that you experienced or witnessed, that you don not take things personally. If you need to clarify the message you are seeing, do it when the receiver will be receptive and not feel threatened.

There is nothing more fun to watch than someone who is smiling because they are happy with their performance or something that they accomplished. As the saying is ... "it's written all over their face," and

3. *Written Communication:* Emails, Facebook, Twitter, text messages and old fashioned written notes, are all forms of written communication. The biggest downfall of this type of communication is, that you can not take the words back once they are delivered. How many times have you pushed the send button and said to yourself, "oh oh."

A lot of your work in this workbook will be written communication to yourself. You are working with yourself on improving your mental training skills through the completion of written activities, so be nice to yourself.

Notes:

Communication

Communicating and Youth

It is sometimes hard to for children to say what they want because they may not know all of the words to describe their message. It can be very frustrating for young badminton players when they feel like they are not being heard. That iss when non-verbal communication might be used more in the form of actions and reactions that might not even have anything to do with what they are trying to get across. I encourage youngsters to experiment and to try not to explain with too many words. Short and simple is the best way to prevent any confusion.

Communication and the Adolescent

It is not easy for adolescents to trust adults or even each other at times. During Communication, it is critical that adults do not judge the message and then ask questions if unsure. Parents and coaches need to make sure that adolescents feel comfortable to communicate without feeling afraid of being honest and open. Honesty and openness should be encouraged without repercussions. This will go very far in building relationships

Adult Communication

Most of us have had all of our lives to learn how to communicate. However, that does not mean that we are good at it. The best way to make sure your message is getting to the recipient, is to ask or clarify that they understand. This should be done in a way that does not judge their abilities, but in a way that says you are just wanting to make sure you communicated the message correctly. You would be amazed at how appreciative others are when you do not blame them for not understanding the message.

Practice Makes You Better

You will definitely get better at communicating with conscious effort. However, you can not control the experience of the recipient, but you can ask questions and learn to be aware of your body language or non verbal communication as much as your verbal communication. Be open to feedback and try to understand if someone is having difficulty getting the message. Be patient and creative if you need to.

Notes:

Communication

Complete the following exercises:

Listening

Describe how listening skills can effect a conversation. Why is it important to:

Focus on how others see the situation. ......

To allow others to finish what they are saying .....

To be non-judgmental .....

To let others express their feelings .....

Speaking Clearly

Describe why it is important to:

Say your exact feelings, thoughts and ideas

Staying Expressive

Discuss why it is important to:

Encourage fellow athletes during practice and games (being supportive and positive ....)

Body Language and Verbal Communication

Describe how body language and verbal communication might effect the way that people could interpret what you are saying.

Notes:

Self-Talk

Are you aware of how you talk to yourself during competition and training? Are you aware of how you talk to yourself in your daily life?

Self-talk is something I bet you actually do every day. I challenge you to be aware of your thoughts for one day. You would be surprised at the things that you say. It is something that just happens naturally. There are probably good and not so good things that you say to yourself all the time.

During games, your self-talk can have a huge effect on your next action. If you tell yourself how bad you are at a skill, chances are you will prove that to yourself when the opportunity presents itself. Sometimes it can become a habit to tell yourself how poorly you are doing. We learn how to talk to ourselves from our environment which most times focuses on the things that need to be improved instead of the things that you are doing well. Consistently telling your self to "get it right" is not useful if you are not addressing specific things about your skill that you want to get right. The side effect of a discussion like this is that it may be more destructive than positive. With those words you can decrease your confidence all on your own without anyone else's assistance.

The goals of the activities included in this book are to help you to become aware of how you talk to yourself and if needed, to change the negative self-talk into positive self-talk. For example changing a sentence like "I can't do this" to "I am going to get this by ....." This change of focus to a more productive one is designed to have you moving forward away from the event that caused you to talk negatively to yourself in the first place.

We learn how to talk to ourselves by our environment. If you have grown up hearing negative things about your skills and abilities it will be your natural response when you make an error or if you don't have a good performance. Your ability to adjust your self-talk after a negative comment, will depend on your history with negative feedback. Start small. The last thing you want is to be talking to yourself negatively because you are not changing your negative self talk fast enough.

When you have gained experience and some consistency in your positive self-talk, use these tips to make self-talk work for you the best way you can.

1. be positive
2. be honest
3. be specific

1. Be Positive

There are many great positive words that you can use during your self-talk. Following are some examples that you can use.

perfect amazing	great	awesome	well done	nicely done
nice work	beautiful	brilliant	excellent	fabulous
outstanding	terrific	superb	quick	wonderful

If you use any negative words to talk to yourself during training or competition, try to replace those negative words with some positive ones. It will not be easy at first. You might only be able to replace the word without including specific instructions. Experiment with different situations so that you can learn to make adjustments automatically. Try it with non badminton situations as well. You will find your new skills very useful for almost any situation.

Notes:

Self-Talk

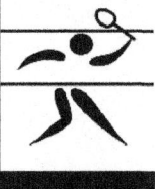

2. Be Honest

It does not help you to tell yourself you are doing great if you are struggling with a skill. Try to be honest about your performance so that you can move forward and improve instead of feeling better for a moment, and then finding yourself having to say the same thing again because you are not getting better.

An example is if you just served the shuttle into the net. And, instead of addressing it as a bad serve, think about your history with serving. If you always miss the target, you want to say "I will get the angle of my racquet right" or "stop, focus, take time and don't rush" If you are good at serving and you miss then you could refer to the distraction that just happened and what you will do if it happens again. This approach is much more productive.

3. Be Specific

The most common thing we hear when someone makes an error is, "nice try" or "you'll get it next time." I believe that is not quite good enough. It is more useful to say something to yourself more like, "next time snap your wrist." or " that was a good reaction, now look at the spot on the floor next time."

It is like you need to be your own coach. Positive specific feedback is much more productive than words that sound nice but are without real meaning. If you are not used to using this kind of process now, you will learn how to make it automatic if you consciously practice it.

Always On

Self-talk is something we do all of the time. Use these guidelines in your daily life and it will be even easier in badminton. It does take practice but this can become as automatic as negative self talk if you can be aware and find opportunities to use it.

Use the self-talk sheet and the record sheet to become more aware of how you talk to yourself and to monitor your interactions with yourself. Learn how to change negative statements to positive ones. Record your progress in the pages provided for notes and use the journal to write down comments or things you want to remember.

Always try to look for the positive in things even when it is hard. If you are finding it hard, let someone know you are having trouble with it and maybe they can help you to make sure the words you are saying to yourself are productive and positive.

Self - Talk for Youth

As youngsters begin to learn skills for self-regulation, self-talk will be one of the things they naturally gravitate to. It is possible that they already talk to themselves in some situations, so it is a good idea to find an opportunity. and ask them how they feel about it. Ask if they have any thoughts or ideas about what self-talk is. Pick small amounts of time to experiment and allow questions. Maybe even ask questions that are easy to understand like, "what would be a good thing to say to yourself in this situation?" Youth are smarter than some give them credit for.

Let them try to purposefully use self-talk with your guidance.

Notes:

Self-Talk

Self - Talk for Adolescents

No matter what sport you are in, there is a good chance you have had some discussions with yourself by now. This might have been at school, with friends or during a badminton game. One of the things that creates negative self-talk is self perception, and imagining what others might think of you. Take some time to reflect on situations where you felt like things were not going well. It is these times more than when things are going great that most will experience self-talk. Write those times down in the notes sections and see if you can replace the statements with positive ones. Find times when you have spoken positively to yourself as well and make note of them.

Self-Talk for Adults

As an adult, you have a whole life time of talking to yourself. In so many situations you have likely said negative things and hopefully positive things as well. Being nice to yourself is a habit, a good habit. Be aware of how you talk or think to yourself in different situations. If you say something positive to yourself make a note of it. If you say something negative make a note of it as well and then make another note of it turned into a positive statement. Everyone deserves to feel good.

Practice Makes You Better

Self-talk is something that's built on what we are used to. If we are from an environment that is critical and judgmental, then we will be the same way with ourselves. Take a look at how your skills or actions have been described by others, especially family, and you'll see how you naturally talk to yourself. The key is to make your statements to yourself the way that you would like to be spoken to. If you are working on badminton skills, you might have some choice words if you are "slacking" or you may let yourself know that you know how to do something that you are having trouble with. Use productive words instead of negative words that are about you personally and make them about your skill specifically. Take opportunities to practice positive self-talk during your day and especially when you are on the badminton court.

Notes:

Self-Talk

24

Write examples of negative things that you say to yourself:

In General:
statement:

ie: "Get it right!"

how do you feel after:

ie: "I can't do it, I'm no good"

During Practice:
statement:

ie: "I can't learn anything"

how you feel after:

ie: stupid, hopeless

During Games:
statement:

ie: "I always choke!"

how you feel after:

ie: "I might as well not be here"

Write a positive statement for each negative one above:

In General:
new statement:

ie: "it's O.K., no one is perfect"

now how do you feel:

ie: I feel like I don't have to know everything

During Practice:
new statement:

ie: "I can learn by my mistakes"

now how do you feel

ie: I feel like I can try it again learning from my mistake

During Games:
new statement

ie: "take a breath"

now how do you feel

ie: nice and easy, no problem

Write down how you think this can affect your performance:

What kind of cues can you use for thought stopping:

Notes:

Self-Talk Record Sheet

25

Record some self-talk that you have said during games & practices and how it affected you : (was it negative? did you need to change it?)

Date: _____ Situation: _____

Statement (or thought): _____

Results: _____

Was there any improvement?: _____

Date: _____ Situation: _____

Statement (or thought): _____

Results: _____

Was there any improvement?: _____

Date: _____ Situation: _____

Statement (or thought): _____

Results: _____

Was there any improvement?: _____

Date: _____ Situation: _____

Statement (or thought): _____

Results: _____

Was there any improvement?: _____

Comments

_____

_____

Notes:

Relaxation

Relaxation skills can be simply taking a deep breath, and letting all of the air in your lungs out while consciously feeling your shoulders relax as you tell yourself it's aaaaaaaaaall goooood. Keeping things in perspective, means that there are other things in life besides this one moment if this one moment happens to be causing you the most anxiety. Just competing and going to the competition can be stressful for you if you are new, or if it is an important one. Butterflies are sometimes a part of competing no matter what the level is that you are playing at. Being able to relax and calm yourself, will be an important skill in your preparation and ability to enjoy your experience no matter what level you are competing at.

Whether you feel it or not, If you are anxious or tense, it will effect your physical reactions enough to have an effect on your skills. Not to mention the psychological effect it can have when a quick decision needs to be made on the court. This emphasizes the importance of being able to not only remove anxiety but to keep a calm outlook on things.

Before Competition

On game day, you might be feeling nervous, and have butterflies in your stomach as you think about how you will perform. You would be amazed at how relaxation can take away some of the anxiety. It can allow you to use positive self-talk to re focus your energy to having fun and getting better at your skills instead of failing. Being able to relax and focus on your abilities and how much fun you are going to have, is important not only for playing the best that you can, but also to enjoying the experience. You need to remember why you are playing badminton, and that is because you love it.

After an Error

Errors are a part of competition. It's how you handle the errors and move to the next play will determine the effect that the error has on the next play. Being able to relax will let you use the tools, like cue-words, to re-focus on the next opportunity.

Before Execution

Taking a breath before executing a skill will take tension away from your muscles and mind, and allow you to focus on executing the skill. Practice relaxation so that it only takes a few seconds to get to that comfortable place again where you are ready to play.

Relaxation is also an important skill to using other mental training skills. If you are tense, your body and mind is more focused on the things that are making you tense than the things that can help you to relax and perform well.

Relaxation with breathing

Breathing is the quickest and most common way to relax. The first thing you will hear someone say to someone who is upset or stressed out is, "breaaaathe" That is because it is the first thing we forget to do when we are stressed. You will also see players, when they are just about to execute a big skill like serving for the game point, they will take a big breath and you can see their shoulders rise up and then down before they prepare.

Breathing is one of the easiest and most used skills and is used for many reasons before, after and during skill execution in almost every sport.

Notes:

Relaxation

Visual Relaxation

Imagine being on a beach with the sun shining and the ocean in front of you. I bet you just took a breath and said to yourself, nice. It probably made you relax instantly. It does for many people that are visual people. During a badminton match, this tool is great for re-focusing after an error or after something distracting that just happened. Seeing your last great performance or something that relaxes you will allow you to calm yourself and use your mental training skills to move on to the next play with confidence.

Relaxation Through Sound

It is true. Some sounds are relaxing. Imagine the sound of the ocean with the sight of the sun and the beach. Relaxed yet? I bet you are. The sound of nice music, and even the sound of quiet can be relaxing. Experiment with things and see how they make you feel and what makes you feel relaxed.

Youth and Relaxation

Youth might not have developed the abilities to focus on sound or visualization even though the might already imagine things all the time. The best way to work with relaxation and youth would be to use breathing. Have them attempt to feel themselves relaxing. It may not be easy since they are becoming aware of their bodies and physiological reactions. Give them lots of time to practice under only recently becoming familiar and various conditions. This will give children a great foundation as they explore other ways to relax. Let them guide some of the relaxation activities and see what they come up with. I am sure you will be surprised.

Adolescence and Relaxation

Many times adolescence will first display nervous laughter when trying to consciously relax using activities in a group setting, this is natural. Eventually though, it will get easier and easier. It is a good idea to practise the skills on alone or in private if it's more comfortable. When it becomes easy, work with a group as well. If you are a coach, let your players know in advance you will be working on relaxation so they can mentally prepare for the session.

Relaxation Skills as an Adult

You likely have had many experiences where you had to relax because of a stressful situation, or maybe you are already good at relaxation. Sometimes the challenge as an adult is to allow yourself to try new things if you feel good about the tools you already use. I challenge you to try all of the relaxation activities that follow, and see if any of them might be a good addition to the strategies you use now.

Sometimes it is difficult however to relax if you do not have any previous experience. Breathing is the easiest way to learn how to relax. By trying the different forms of relaxation, you will definitely find at least one form that works best for you. Experiment under different situations and you will find that when you need it, it will be easier than you think.

Notes:

Relaxation

Practise Makes You Better

It can take you as little as five seconds to relax when you are good at the techniques that you are most comfortable with. The best time in badminton to be good at relaxation skills of course is during competition, when you need to re focus on something after being distracted in some way. This tool will also be great in your day to day activities as you come across stressful situations or anxiety at work or at home.

Try the relaxation exercises as you feel comfortable, and then record some of your experiences in the notes pages. You will find that as you gain experience with the different ways to relax, it will become easier and easier to relax when you need it the most.

Notes:

Relaxation (part 1)

29

Try the following relaxation techniques alone or with someone else:
(record your thoughts and feelings after each exercise)

The 5 - to - 1 count
- say the number 5 to yourself, and take a full, slow breath as you focus on the number 5
- exhale fully and completely (getting the last bit of air out of the lungs is important)
- count 4 and inhale slowly
- say "I am more relaxed now than I was at number 5" as you exhale
  (exhale fully and completely - DO NOT RUSH YOUR THOUGHTS)
- count 3 and inhale slowly
- say "I am more relaxed now than I was at number 4" as you exhale fully and completely
- count 2 and inhale slowly
- say "I am more relaxed now than I was at number 3" as you exhale fully and completely
- feel the deepening relaxation
- feel calmer and more relaxed as you approach number 1

Feelings / Thoughts:

_____

_____

Three - Part - Breathing
- take a deep breath from your diaphragm
- imagine that your lungs are divided into three parts - upper, middle, and lower
- imagine the lower part of your lungs filling with air, use only your diaphragm when you breath
  your chest should remain almost still
- imagine the middle part of your lungs filling with air, as you see this expansion let your rib
  cage move forward a bit
- imagine the upper part of your lungs filling with air and your lungs becoming completely
  full, let your shoulders rise slightly and move backward
- exhale fully and completely, as you empty the upper part of your lungs drop your shoulders
  slightly, see the air leaving the middle part of your lungs and feel your rib cage contract, pull
  your abdomen in to force the last bit of air from the bottom of your lungs
- repeat the above sequence four times

Feelings / Thoughts:

_____

_____

Notes:

Relaxation (part 2)

30

Visual Controlled Breathing

- close your eyes
- see your body in a comfortable, relaxed position
- inhale slowly, and see your chest fill with air
- hold it momentarily
- exhale slowly, and release air steadily through your mouth and nose
- feel the release of tension / anxiety

Feelings / Thoughts:

_____

_____

Kinesthetic Controlled Breathing

- close your eyes
- feel your stomach move out; keep the chest and shoulders steady
- slowly inhale, feeling the increase of air in the chest and a rise of the shoulder
- hold it
- slowly exhale, feeling a release in tension as the shoulders and chest drop and the stomach relaxes

Feelings / Thoughts:

_____

_____

Audio Controlled Breathing

- close your eyes
- hear yourself slowly inhale and exhale air as you breathe
- slowly inhale
- hear the air pass through your mouth and nose
- feel the build-up of tension
- slowly release the air
- hear the sound of air passing through your nose and mouth

Feelings / Thoughts

_____

_____

Used with Permission from the Coaching Association of Canada

Notes:

Relaxation Review

After looking over the breathing techniques and your comments, record how you feel about the one or ones that you think would work best for you and in what situations you can use them.

If you have discovered your own technique, write it down and describe in what situations you can best use it.

Technique:

Comments

_____

_____

Situations to use it

_____

_____

Technique:

Comments

_____

_____

Situations to use it

_____

_____

Technique:

Comments

_____

_____

Situations to use it

_____

_____

Notes:

Concentration

Concentration is the action or power of focusing one's attention or mental effort on one specific thing. The ability to execute a skill and focus on what you are doing in a distracting situation is very important to success in badminton. Spectators, supporters, teammates, coaches, opponents, and officials are all potential distractions during competition. The other distraction though could be yourself. Your self-talk and ability to zone in on what needs to be done can in itself be a distraction.

Distraction Control

The number of potential distractions during a game can be huge. They can take your attention away from what needs to be done. You can also be distracted by something that happened during the day, or maybe you are feeling nervous about being new to badminton. From the beginner to the elite, the potential for distractions are the same, even though the magnitude and potential consequences might not be.

If you are new to badminton, you might be distracted by your skill level, and say to yourself, "What if I screw up?" It is important that you learn to refocus that thought process back into the game that you want to enjoy with your friends. The use of mental skills, like cue words and relaxation, can be very helpful in concentration. Elite and competitive athletes might be dealing with an international competition where the results will determine of they will qualify for the Olympics. Even though this is likely than you are at, the emotional effect it can have is many times the same.

Focusing and re-focusing is a skill that when mastered can be one of the best tools for staying "in the game." Someone calling your name or the sound of a child crying because they are hungry or tired in the stands can take you right out of your zone pretty quick. Having skills such as looking at a spot somewhere on the court, and re-zoning your thoughts into the game is something that takes practise. Picking up the shuttle for example and tossing it in the air can allow you to focus on it and regroup your thoughts. Acknowledging the distraction, and then consciously re-directing your focus will help if it happens again.

Concentration

How do you use concentration to deal with distractions? How many times have you heard someone say to just concentrate. Well you have probably thought to yourself that it is easier said than done. What is concentration? It's almost the same as focussing, but it is for a specific event. An example would be if you are in an important game like a final or a semi final, and there is a semi final also happening on the court beside you. Being able to concentrate on serving and not how your opponent will respond while there is cheering and noise beside you.

Concentration can be even more difficult for a recreational badminton player depending on your skill level, because there can be so many things to distract you, including your own skills. Add the confidence factor and it might even be more difficult. If you are confident in your skills or athletic abilities, then you will probably find it easier to keep your concentration than it is if you don not have confidence.

Focus

The ability to keep your focus on a specific task or object is <u>concentration</u>. The ability to move that concentration to something else while still concentrating, is considered <u>focus</u>. They go together and are equally important to success in badminton.

Notes:

Concentration

There are four types of focus, and they all work together depending on the situation and what you are concentrating on at that moment.

1. Internal Focus: this focusing is sort of kinesthetic or the feeling type of focus. Actually feeling the movement in your muscles, or concentrating on how you are physically feeling is internal focus. Internal focus is also focusing on your thoughts about something that might have happened. This is a type of focus used when you are learning badminton skills or in a stressful situation where you have to do something specific. For example, trying to feel how your arm and wrist move while returning a serve, or feeling the strength of your shoulders and arms as smash the shuttle to the ground on your opponents side. During competition, you would probably not be trying to feel the skill but you would definitely experience internal focus when thinking about the skill or planning your strategy.

2. External Focus: is focusing attention outward on an object that is in front of you like the shuttle. This focus is used when striking as your racquet is meeting the shuttle to serve or on a return after your opponent serves.

3. Narrow Focus is focusing on something specific like where you want the shuttle to land after you hit it. This is when your focus is only on relevant cues that could effect the goal such as the quickness of your opponent and where they are on the court. Your ability to keep this focus can be effected by distractions around you and your psychological arousal level. If you are not mentally focused enough, you can be distracted by surrounding cues or activity. If you are too focused, you might miss important cues such as the opponent moving just before your racquet meets the shuttle.

4. Broad Focus: is focusing on more than one thing at one time. This would be something like focusing during doubles and being aware of where each opponent is on the court. Sometimes the specific situation will determine where your focus is such as if you are delivering or receiving the shuttle. If you are receiving, you need to know where your team mate is and the lines of the court. If you are delivering, you need to know where both opponents are and the lines on the court.

During competition and training, it's common to be using two types of focus at one time. Some of them sound the same but have very different meanings. Some of these combinations are as follows:

1. Narrow / Internal Focus: is focusing on something specific that you are doing like focusing on the spot on the floor (narrow) and keeping calm (internal) while smashing the shuttlecock down to the floor at the same time. This focus will be used often in badminton although you might not be consciously thinking of it as narrow/internal focus. By just being aware of it will be helpful. When learning new skills, you will use narrow internal focus while trying to feel your body executing the skill at the same time as you are focusing on the outcome that you are trying to achieve.

2. Narrow / External Focus: is focusing only on something specific outside of your body awareness such as a target only (narrow) and the surrounding events (external) at the same time. For example you might be at a tournament and hear the spectators or opponents while trying to focus on where you want the shuttle to land. Use simulation activities to give you experience with the stressors in this type of situation.

Notes:

Concentration

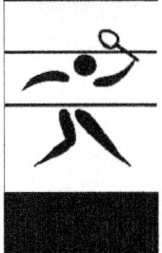

3. <u>Broad / Internal Focus</u>: is being aware of multiple things that are happening in the environment (broad) while focusing on your breathing to relax in the situation and executing the mechanics of a skill (internal). This can be difficult without practise. Being aware of your breathing for example will help you to call on this skill quickly during competition. This focus will mostly be used for emotional control and in preparation for a skill such as serving because of the precision that is needed.

4. <u>Broad / External Focus</u>: is focusing on things happening outside of what you are doing (broad) and the sport equipment that you are using such as the shuttle. Moving around your team mate in doubles while getting to the shuttle is broad/external focus.

Concentration and Focus for Youth

Children have so much going on that it can be hard for them to concentrate or focus all of the time. Give them something they enjoy and you will see concentration at the highest level. Keep their activities simple without too much discussion and they will slowly learn skills at their own pace. Too often we tell youth to concentrate, but do not teach them how to concentrate. It is important to involve them in the process. They may know exactly what is happening but might not understand it as well as an adult. Of course this is because they do not have the experience and knowledge of life that we do either. We need to remember that.

Give them small and easy to accomplish activities that need focus and then eventually put the activities together. Allowing them to flow into the idea of re-focusing. Allow them to work together on focusing and concentration strategies. You would be amazed at how they work their way through these skills with each other. Youth can be much more creative then adults some times so we need to give them more credit for their abilities.

Concentration and Focussing for Adolescents

This can be a very challenging task for badminton players who have so much going on in their physiological and psychological development. It is important to be aware of, and allow players to move into being on the court or training location from the environment that they are arriving from. Give them lots of opportunities to refine these skills and to experiment with different strategies.

Concentration and Focusing for Adults

As adults, we have many experiences and have maybe even experimented with concentration strategies. Our ability to focus has been established already and is easier to put into action when executing a task. It is not easy though, when we add anxiety or stress, or if something else is going on in our lives that has nothing to do with badminton. This is when it is good to have skills that allow you to re-focus from the day and back onto the court and enjoying badminton with your friends or even at an international event.

You may have to concentrate all day at your job and just want to relax and have fun playing badminton. Consciously knowing that is believe it or not, a help to actually making it happen. Being able to re-focus your energy on not being stressed out about performance, and enjoying badminton instead of getting anxious can actually take concentration.

Notes:

Concentration

Practise Makes You Better

Take some time and experiment with the different types of focus and see if you can identify them. Use the activities in the book to improve your concentration and focusing skills. Skills like relaxation and self talk that you learned in earlier activities in this book will help you as you continue to get better at concentration, focusing and re-focusing.

Notes:

Concentration / Focusing

Write down five situations in badminton where concentration is needed and what can happen if you are not focused (try to be specific).

(this exercise is to become aware of how concentration is important in badminton, or in any activity).

Situation

ie: expecting a drive return after a serve, I stay back in my court

Result

ie: a deep high serve is returned with a net shot that hits the floor

Situation

Result

Situation

Result

Situation

Result

Notes:

Re-Focusing

Using relaxation and concentration / focusing techniques that you learned in the practices up until now, try to "re-focus" your attention when someone or something is distracting you.

Work with a group of 4 for this exercise.

Set up on a court so that you are rallying as singles, each pair having half of the court
- 1 person counts the number of times the player beside you hits the shuttle
- use your sight and sound senses
- the partner who is not counting keeps the time for 2 minutes
- the player who is being counted for, counts the number of times he/she hits the shuttle
- after 2 minutes, compare numbers then rotate
- to increase difficulty, count for both players beside you

Discuss with each other the techniques you used to re-focus on the shuttle while checking on the player beside you.

Techniques you used and how they worked for you:

_____

_____

_____

_____

Techniques your partner used that you might try:

_____

_____

_____

_____

Now try it again
Discuss with others what techniques worked for you to stay focused and re-focus on the task at hand.

Some techniques others used that you might try:

_____

_____

_____

_____

Notes:

Concentration Exercises 38

Concentration on a clock face
1. Concentrate on the second hand of a watch or clock as it goes all the way around one time. Blink your eyes or snap your fingers every five seconds.
2. After the second hand goes around once, concentrate on the moving hand as it goes all the way around again. This time blink your eyes or snap your fingers every ten seconds.
3. After the second hand goes around twice, concentrate on the moving hand as it goes around a third time. This time, alternate blinking your eyes and snapping your fingers every five seconds.

Shuttling
1. Choose a partner
2. If you go first, close your eyes, tune in to some sensation, feeling, or thought, and say something like "Now I am aware of a pain in my leg". "Now I am aware of my breathing", or "Now I am feeling silly".
3. Then open your eyes and say "Now I am aware ...." adding something that is happening outside yourself. For instance, say "Now I am aware of the sunlight" or "Now I am aware of your eyes".
4. Repeat the process - first an inside statement, then an outside one - for a few minutes without a break. If you get stuck, the partner should help you out by asking, "Now I am aware of .....?".
5. Your partner now does the concentration exercise.
6. After both of you have tried it, try the exercise with your eyes open the whole time.

Stopping Thoughts
1. Sit quietly, close your eyes, relax, and think of a situation that causes negative thoughts that have affected your performance.
2. Sense the feeling and actions that go with these negative thoughts.
3. Think "stop" as they happen and immediately replace negative thoughts with more positive ones. Sense the feelings and actions that go with these new thoughts.
4. Think about how the feelings and actions were different and how this experience relates to a competitive situation.

Using the situations and results page as a reference, go back and describe how these exercises can help you with the situations that you recorded.

Comments:

_____

_____

_____

Notes:

Cue Words

39

Try this, think of a word that has more meaning to it than the word itself. For example, you might say "game" which might mean re-focus back on the court and listen for sounds of the game and your opponent or teammate, to stop the things outside of the game from distracting you. You might also use cue words for skill execution. "Quick" might be a word that you could use to remind yourself to get to the line to return a shuttle that has been hit hard to the back of the court.

Most people are talking to themselves more than they realize. So consciously talking to yourself can be helpful in badminton, and can then even transfer over to your daily activities as well. How many times have you been in a tense situation at work or amongst friends and said to yourself, "it's ok." which might mean to put things in perspective because it is not that important. Using a cue word as simple as "breathe" can let you to take a second to calm yourself.

You might also use cue words sometimes without even knowing it. You may use a word like "keys" to tell yourself to make sure you put them in the same spot all the time so that you always know where to get them when you need them. You can do the same thing here.

Using a single word to remind you of a few things you want to remember in a badminton skill is helpful during competition and training. They can also be used in helping you with relaxing when you are anxious. You might use a word like "breath" to remind yourself to relax your shoulders and take a big breath and let the air out slowly to calm yourself.

You might also use a word to help when you are learning a new technical or tactical skill to remind yourself of what you have to do during the execution. Something to remind you of posture or extending your arm for the smash.

Cue words do not only need to be actual words. They can also be images that represent a cue such as a stop sign or a green light. I have for example used traffic light colours to help athletes learn about their emotional control and to be able to change their emotions based on the colour of the traffic light. This worked great during games when I could just say the colour to remind the team to breathe and calm down during an important competition.

After an Error

It is common to experience negative self-talk after an error. You can devise cue words though, that will help you to get back on track and to get rid of the negative feeling that often come with negative events. There are many words that players use such as "STOP" if they are thinking of bad things. or alternatively seeing a stop sign. The idea of flushing a negative thought is another common tool. Practise with different words or images and set one that you can use anytime that you need it.

For Learning Skills

Sometimes it is hard to learn a new sports skill, especially if it is complicated and there are many parts to it. By creating cue words for remembering a specific part of a skill, you can remind yourself of how to move when executing the skill in a drill at practise or training. It's important to keep the word simple and not complicated, especially if the skill is complicated.

Notes:

Cue Words

40

During Competition

You might find that you are nervous or anxious before executing a badminton skill, or just before the game. This anxiety can be even stronger before an important game. A cue word can help you to relax and put everything into perspective even before leaving for the court. Taking a deep breath and just saying something like, "relax" or "its all good" can help you to calm yourself and enjoy the moment and focusing on the process instead of being tense and uneasy about the potential outcome which you have no real control over.

Cue Words for Youth

Youth need to have simple words with simple meanings. Observe the actions and reactions to see how children are responding to potentially stressful events and guide them to find words that help them to relax and calm themselves. It is very important to remember that it is their process and they need to build it instead of adults building it for them. This will help to develop their abilities to work with cue words on their own later in sport. The sense of empowerment will also motivate them in their journey.

Cue Words for Adolescents

As we know, many adolescents have their own language. Allow adolescence to use their words that have meaning to them in developing their own cue words. Help them to become aware of how words can effect their energy levels and abilities to control their emotions. It is a growing process and adults need to allow teenagers to achieve results individually.

Cue Words for Adults

As adults, you may have already developed cue words over the years. Try to catch yourself using a word for something and see how it makes you feel and how effective it is. You might find that you need to make some changes to them so that they are more useful in sport and training.

Practise Makes Better

Use the notes pages and experiment with different words. You might change them or you might find some that work right away. Use them in badminton and learn how to give them the effect that they are designed for.

Notes:

Cue's & Cue Words

41

Choose some words that will help you to focus on thoughts that you want to remember in a badminton skill:

Skill Related Cue Words

<u>Example:</u>

shuffle — to remember to side-step to move to a shuttle to my left or right

cross — to remember to use the cross-step to get a shuttle to the side

<u>Cue Word</u> <u>Skill</u>

Why are Cue words important in a game?

What kind of physical, mental or technical cues can you pick up from the opponents to help you?

ie: your opponent is tiring

advantage: not as aggressive so I should make him/her move around more

Notes:

Cue Words

42

Match the words with the desired results

Energy Related Cue Words

crush
force
quick   a   calmness
press
sprint   b   strength
feeling good
intense   c   power
blast
rip   d   speed
fast
drive   e   agility
magnificent
explode   f   persistence
scoot
zoom   g   confidence
breath
easy   h   balance
superb

Others for badminton specifically

Notes:

Visualization

I bet you visualize more than you know. Visualization can be used for skill development, relaxation, focusing, concentrating, regaining or maintaining composure. There are five types of effective visualization as you will see in this workbook. Experiment with all of them and use them in your different situations.

1. Visual

Seeing is like imagining. It is not easy for everyone to see this way or to imagine this way. A good way to practice is to take an object, look at it, then close your eyes and try to see it in your mind with your eyes closed. Use an object like a badminton racquet with bright colours and it will be easier. This skill is great for learning and rehearsing technical and tactical skills. It is also useful for imagining being in the big game by using your mental training skills to concentrate.

2. Auditory

The sound of the racquet hitting the shuttle, is an amazing sound when it is done well. As with seeing an object, you can rehearse using sound as well. Play a noise on your iPod or listen to something on your TV and then hit the mute button while trying to hear it as it just sounded. Practise hearing specific things during the day and see if you can repeat the sound in your mind. When preparing for an important event, use a recording of spectators to help you to prepare for the noises you will hear.

3. Kinesthetic

Actually feeling the skill takes practice and awareness of your body. A good way to practice this skill is to close your eyes and move your body. Use your badminton racquet and a shuttle and feel the weight of the object and how it feels to move it around. Make sure that there is nobody in the immediate vicinity for safety purposes.

Smell

This one should be somewhat easy. What is your favourite food? We might not use this skill in our development, but it could be useful if you are going to be competing in an environment that has a specific smell to it like being close to the sea or in a hot building. By being familiar and rehearsing, it will give you familiarity before arriving at the venue.

Taste

This skill is also not one that you will likely be using in your preparations. It is a way however to become aware of your senses which is never a bad thing. Unless of course your sport is the annual hot dog eating contest.

Visualization for Youth

Youth use unstructured imagination all of the time. Mention an ice cream cone; their favourite snack or going to their favourite amusement park and watch their eyes light up. Working with children gently, and showing them how they are actually using visualization will help in using the skills later in sport. They will respond more readily to the word "imagine" better than the word "visualize" because they use the word imagine often when interacting with each other. Allow them to be creative and minimize limitations on their imagination.

Notes:

Visualization

Visualization for Adolescents

Using the word imagine instead of visualize is a good start when someone is not familiar with the actual term visualization. Every teenager imagines something I bet. Even if it is being at the beach with their friends or going to a movie and other activities with friends. Experiment with the different types of visualization to find the one that works best and that can be used to improve mental training skills.

Visualization for Adults

We have a whole life time of imagination to draw on. When you think back on an event, many times you will actually see the event and sometimes even remember the smells and feelings surrounding the event. Experiment with conscious and directed visualization, and try it during games and training sessions if you are not familiar with it.

Practice Makes Better

If you have difficulty visualizing, use every opportunity to practice and try it. Even if you are watching TV, close your eyes and try to see the picture you were just looking at. Use your imagination to create things. Take the time to use the exercises in this book to improve your abilities to visualize or, imagine.

If you are having a bad day competing or training, try to use visualization to bring yourself to a better and more productive place. Relaxation will be a big help with visualization because it will calm your mind so that you can focus on what you are trying to see, hear, smell, feel or taste.

Use this skill to help your competition. Try to be specific in your visualizations. Try to see, feel and hear the activity from beginning to end. It will definitely improve your skills without even touching the court floor.

The best time to visualize is before going to sleep and/or when you first get up because your mind is the most quiet. Give it a try.

Notes:

Visualization

Try the following visualization exercises
>   - be sure to visualize correct technique for specific skills
>   - after you have completed each exercise, write down your thoughts
>   (was it easy or hard to visualize, did you find your mind wandering?)

Exercise 1 (seeing through visualization)
Imagine the empty court with no one in the area .....
Imagine a shuttlecock sitting on the floor .....
Imagine you rallying in a warmup .....
Imagine you set up to serve in a game .....
Imagine you executing a perfect smash on the opponents return .....
Imagine you dropping the shuttle for the point .....

Thoughts:

_____

_____

Exercise 2 (hearing through visualization)
Imagine the sound of the playing area while getting prepared .....
Imagine the sound of spectators .....
Imagine the sound of your racquet hitting the shuttlecock .....
Imagine the sound of the shuttlecock hitting the floor .....
Imagine the sound of your fans calling out encouragement .....
Imagine the sound of the whistle before you serve .....

Thoughts:

_____

_____

Exercise 3 (physically feeling through visualization)
Imagine the feel of the feathers on a shuttle .....
Imagine the feel of the strings on your badminton racquet .....
Imagine the feel of smashing the shuttle .....
Imagine the feel of the racquet in your hand .....
Imagine the feel of the base of the shuttle as you are preparing to serve .....

Thoughts:

_____

_____

Notes:

Visualization

Exercise 4 (smelling through visualization)

Imagine the smell of a new leather glove .....
Imagine the smell of a newly strung racquet .....
Imagine the smell of an old leather glove .....
Imagine the smell of your favorite dinner cooking on the stove .....

Thoughts:

_____

_____

Exercise 5 (tasting through visualization)

Imagine the taste of your favorite dinner that you just smelled .....
Imagine the taste of a dry mouth when you are thirsty .....
Imagine the taste of salty chips .....
Imagine the taste of a favorite beverage after a tough game ......

Thoughts:

_____

_____

How did the different types of visualization affect you and how will they come in handy during games?
Write down any new ideas that you may get:
ie: I can see myself executing my backhand perfectly

_____

_____

_____

_____

_____

_____

_____

_____

_____

_____

Notes:

Visualization for Games

Put yourself in a situation where the competition is at a very important point. *(ie. you are near the end of an important game, you are up by 2 points and you are tiring)*, how can you use visualization to help you concentrate in this situation?

_____

_____

_____

Put yourself in a common situation that you sometimes have trouble with during a competition *(ie. getting back into ready position after making a shot)*, visualize the best response that you think should happen in this situation.

_____

_____

_____

Put yourself in a situation that might cause anxiety or stress in during competition *(ie. you don't like the opponent, there are competitors watching you)*, visualize a response that you would find calming or helpful to keep your concentration and energy level productive.

_____

_____

_____

Put yourself in a very tense situation *(ie. someone just said or did something that you found upsetting)*, see if you can use visualization to bring on a calming effect that will keep you focused on the competition and not what just happened.

_____

_____

_____

Notes:

Practice with Visualization

(48)

Seeing and Feeling the Skill

Pick a skill that you have done perfectly *(ie. a short serve)*. As you visualize the skill, first "see" yourself perform the skill and concentrate on important parts of your technique. Concentrating on this part, try to feel the performance.

What skill did you visualize? Were you able to see and feel the skill being performed as perfectly as you have done it before?

_____

_____

_____

_____

Practicing Just Before the Activity

In a practice area, visualize yourself performing a task that you commonly perform in a competitive situation *(ie. a clear shot)*. Try to see yourself performing the skill perfectly as you would want it done during competition. Now actually do the task as you did in your visualization.

Were you able to visualize yourself perfectly? How was your performance after the visualization? How can you use this technique before or during practices or games?

_____

_____

_____

_____

Feeling the Skill

Like the exercise you just did, in a practice area, visualize yourself performing a task that you commonly perform in a competitive situation *(ie. cross-court shot)*. This time try to feel yourself executing the skill perfectly as you would want it performed during competition. Now actually do the task as you did in your visualization.

Were you able to feel yourself performing the skill? How was your performance after the visualization? How can you use this technique before or during practices and games?

_____

_____

_____

_____

Notes:

Visualization During Games

Seeing and Feeling the Skill
Use this technique in a competitive situation and experiment with the results *(ie. on your way back from a timeout, visualize a perfect return).*

What skill did you visualize? Were you able to see and feel the skill being performed as perfectly as you have done before?

_____

_____

_____

_____

Practicing Just Before the Activity
Use this technique in a practice situation and experiment with the results *(ie. just before serving, visualize putting the shuttle exactly where you want it to go).*

What skill did you visualize? Were you able to visualize yourself performing the skill perfectly? How was your performance after the visualization? How can you use this technique before or during practices or competitions?

_____

_____

_____

_____

Feeling the Skill
Use this technique in a practice situation and experiment with the results *(ie. a drive at the opponent).*

What skill did you visualize? Where you able to visualize yourself performing the skill perfectly? How was your performance after the visualization? How can you use this technique before or during practices or competitions?

_____

_____

_____

_____

Notes:

The Controllables

One of the most frustrating things in badminton is the when things are not working your way and you feel like there is nothing that can be done to change it. Officials calls or the opponents can be the perceived cause of distraction and decreased performance in almost any sport.

The key to dealing with these distractions and frustrations is knowing what you have control over and taking that control to make sure that you do not get wrapped up in what you do not have control over.

Opponents

Opponents are something that we do and do not have control over. We can control to a degree their choices in reactions and actions in badminton where you return the shuttle to a specific location causing them to move to that location and chose their swing based on that location. The next part of that action is not in your control. How they actually respond to that return as far as location and depth of their return is now something that you respond to based on how they are attempting to control your action.

In a sport like gymnastics, you have total control of your performance because it is not dependant on the actions or reactions of your opponents. Unlike in badminton, the final score for you depends on your performance only and where it stands in relation to your opponent.

Officials

No one ever has control over how an official calls a game. The only control you have is weather you hit the shuttle out of bounds or into the net. Officials are a common frustration for many but the sooner that you can realize your lack of control over how they view your game, the less frustration you will experience. Officials come from their own backgrounds with their own stresses and levels of experience. All of these things will have an effect on how they call a game. Use your mental training skills to focus and re focus when you are feeling frustrated by a call or a missed call.

Spectators

How many times have you heard comments from spectators that are disrespectful to someone on your team or another player or even towards you. Next time you are at a badminton game, notice the spectators and imagine how you would react if you were a participant at the event. How do you think the actions would be distracting? How can you use mental training skills to keep your emotional control in such a situation?

Coaches

Executing skills without worrying about what the coach is thinking can actually be more of a distraction than a help. By worrying about the coach, your performance will suffer because of anxiety and stress. You ca not control what your coach is thinking, it takes away from your enjoyment of the competition and can add stress and anxiety.

Teammates

We ca not have control over what our teammate in a doubles game does or how they perform. It is important to know the level of control you have if any so that you can prevent any unnecessary stresses. You will have interactions with him/her but you have no control over how they respond.

Sport Environment

You have no control over the sport environment unless you are the one that develops and builds it. The best way to approach this lack of control is to prepare for competing in that environment. For example if you playing in a new facility, know the area, go to the area if possible or get a picture or video of the facility to have some familiarity. Know where the washrooms are and where you can get refreshments. Be aware of the average temperature you will be playing in and if possible, practice in that temperature to be familiar with it. **For safety purposes however do not practice without safety precautions if necessary.**

Sport Equipment

Access to quality equipment is dependant on your budget or the budget of the team or association you are competing for. It is critical that you realize the potential of your equipment and learn to compete within those parameters. For example you might not have an expensive badminton racquet but that does not mean that you are not capable of playing well. If you

Notes:

The Controllables

have a badminton that is not as light as you would like, you just need to have more strength to have the same amount of speed it would produce. Use what you have and play the sport instead of the equipment.

You

Yes, you are a controllable. How you approach your training and competition is going to have the biggest effect on how you improve and enjoy your experience. This is sometimes harder to control than things outside of you that you think you have control over. This sometimes makes it the last thing to be considered when the frustration begins. Use the exercises that you have been learning to this point, to re focus and re claim the things you have control over.

By being as prepared as you can and planning as much as you can, you can minimize how your environment can effect you negatively.

Youth and Controllables

More often than not, youth have no control over most of the things within their sport. I believe it is a good idea to let children experiment with control in badminton so they can develop decision making skills. Safety of course is the number one concern and there are many ways that you can allow control that is safe and effective.

Some great ideas include:

- team rules
- selected team training drills
- selected competitions

I have had great success giving youngsters as young as eight years old control over the things listed above. It is amazing how well they respond to this type of activity that also helps them to begin developing their own self direction as well.

Adolescents and Controllables

I found that there's a fine line between giving too much control and not enough control in this situation. It is critical that teenagers feel they are a part of the process and that they are thought of as contributing members to the their own success. I found that when they felt more in control , they were much more responsive and were more likely to offer assistance with different tasks and developments of the team. It was awesome!

Adults and Controllables

As adults the tendency is to feel like we have more control than we actually do. This task of determining the controllables and working within those parameters is an awesome tool that will let you enjoy your training and competition. Make adjustments as you move through the exercises and then even transfer the skills to your daily life.

Practise Makes You Better

Awareness and practise with controllables is the key to success. Being honest and then taking responsibility for what you have control over such as your own performance skills and your conduct. Your physical, technical and mental training skills can only be improved if you make a decision to improve them.

As you complete the exercises, think of actual situations in badminton where you felt you did or did not have control in a situation. Talk with others and observe what happens in your competitive environment. When the outcome is on the line is usually when people have the hardest time with controllables.

Notes:

The Controllables

Write down inside the square the things that you have control over in badminton. In the outside portion of the square, write down the things that you do not have control over .

Notes:

The Controllables

Write down in the middle of the square some of the things that you have control over in your daily life. In the outside portion of the square, write down some things that you do not have control over .

Notes:

My Control

54

Think of a situation in badminton where you do not have control and a response if the event happens. *(ie. the official calls the shuttle out but it hits the line)*

_____

_____

_____

_____

Think of an emotional situation in badminton where you have control during a game and a response if the event happens. *(ie. someone verbally blames you for a bad play on the court)*

_____

_____

_____

_____

Think of situation in badminton that you have had where you do not have control and you have gotten frustrated and what your new response will be.

_____

_____

_____

_____

_____

_____

Think of a situation in badminton where you were initially frustrated and then realized that it was not in your control. What did you do to relieve the stress. What was the situation?

_____

_____

_____

_____

_____

_____

Notes:

Ideal Performance State

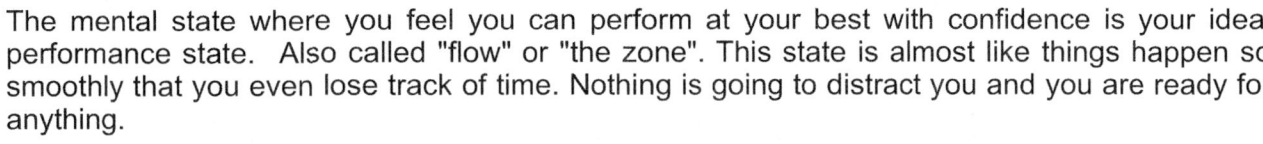

The mental state where you feel you can perform at your best with confidence is your ideal performance state. Also called "flow" or "the zone". This state is almost like things happen so smoothly that you even lose track of time. Nothing is going to distract you and you are ready for anything.

Emotional Control

With so many possibilities for stress in badminton, being able to control emotions is very important to success. Getting to the finals is very exciting, and being able to keep your composure while preparing for competition can be a hard. The first thing that needs to happen is you need to stop! Look around and see where you are. How did you get there and what needs to be done for success in the situation? Now time to relax, re-focus and use your cue words to stay focused and believe in your abilities knowing that you are going to use your mind as well as your body for success, and you are as prepared as you are going to be at that moment.

What about that official you see arriving to the court that you know has missed calls in the past and does not always have control of the game. AAAAAAARRRRGGG!!! Well it is the same thing. Stop, look around and see where you are, how did you get there and what needs to be done for success in the situation. Now time again to relax, re-focus, use your mental training skills and remind yourself of what you have control over.

Game Readiness

Game preparation is crucial to success. Being able to arrive at the facility feeling confident and ready to compete will have a big role in the results at the end of the day. This is where your "Ideal Performance State" comes in. Having a pre-competition routine will give your mind and body a path to getting in the zone no matter what happened during the day leading up to the event. It takes practice to build this path and to be able to maintain it but you will find it very useful once established.

A pre-competition routine can include things like, making sure you have all your gear in your bag and making sure you have eaten before you leave home by having your meal prepared the night before. You would be amazed at how often that is forgotten. Prepare mentally using visualization in the morning or on your way to the competition site while listening to music if you are not driving. Even your pre-game warm up is part of your routine. Use that time to transition into your "Ideal Performance State" leaving your day behind.

Get to know the things that distract you and disrupt your preparations and learn how to deal with them so that they will not be a distraction. This will go a long way in your game preparedness and will be one of your best tools for the most important competitions.

Use the worksheets to help you plan and refine your ideal performance state and then use the planning sheets to set up your routines. Then you can use your other mental training skills that you previously learned to keep and get back to that state and you are all set.

Self Regulation

The ability to control your emotions during training and competition is critical to performance success. There are so many ways to get distracted and many ways that external events can effect your emotions. A bad call, a rivalry with a local competitor, a negative interaction with an opponent. All of these things have a potential to disrupt your ideal performance state or zone. Relaxation, cue

Notes:

Ideal Performance State

words and focusing strategies will help you to put things into perspective and to focus on what you do have control over. You are the one that can effect the outcome and how you respond to your environment.

Stress Management

Rest, recovery and good command of mental training skills will contribute to stress management. Being aware of what causes you stress during training or competition will give you insight into how the skills you learn will help you through those situations as they come up. Experience with the stressor is one of the best ways to prepare. This is also why having as much information about an event and location as you can for an event will be important in your preparations.

The following are some things to consider when preparing for competition.

- location
- weather
- type of food you will be eating
- facility layout
- environment
- information on opponents
- information on officials
- expectations of performance
- importance of competition

Ideal Performance State for Youth

We want youth to enjoy their sport experience. Small introductions to some level of ideal performance state will help them to begin the process. A piece of information such as knowing where they are competing, who they are competing with and that their focus for the competition will help them to prepare mentally. Asking how they feel before a competition and how they would like to feel will begin the process.

Ideal Performance State for Adolescents

There are lots of things in the day that will be distracting for teenage participants. Having a pre-competition preparation plan will help with the transition from school or hanging out with friends to the training or competition. These types of activities will help the mind to prepare for competition or training even if the body is not yet ready.
Using the mental training skills learned up to this point, it will not be hard to prepare a plan and to return back to your ideal performance state if you are distracted.

Ideal Performance State for Adults

We have so many responsibilities in our day. Employment, family, perhaps children and friends. With that comes many distractions to prevent us from being prepared for competition. By completing the exercises and by following a pre competition routine, the transition will be easier and you will be able to move smoothly from your day to the competitive environment.

Notes:

Ideal Performance State

Practise Makes You Better

By writing down notes after games, you can begin to compile useful information and tips for improving your ability to remain and get back to your ideal performance state at any time. This is one of the most difficult mental training tasks in sport. With practice and by using your learned mental training skills it will get easier and will eventually become natural.

The purpose of these last activities and focus in your mental training skills is to give you a tool so that you can have fun and enjoy the process. If you are moving along to more elite mental training, this book will give you a great foundation to continue.

Enjoy the process.

Notes:

Ideal Performance State

58

Recall your best performance

How did it feel?

_____

_____

What was on your mind?

_____

_____

What was your attitude?

_____

_____

What special things do you remember?

_____

_____

Describe the performance (use all of your senses, sight, sound, touch, taste).

_____

_____

_____

_____

_____

What do you need to do technically (what skills do you need) to perform at your best?
   - use descriptive words to list these qualities

_____

_____

_____

_____

Notes:

Ideal Performance State

After your First Competition

Rank your performance on the competition #1 Form
- 1 is high
- 5 is poor

Use key words as a guide to put a number value on your emotional/mental control

Emotional Control	1 =	anxious
	2 =	butterflies
	3 =	calm
	4 =	composed
	5 =	confident

Mental Focus	1 =	focused
	2 =	narrowing *(ie. focusing on the shuttle only)*
	3 =	scanning
	4 =	broadening *(ie. focusing on the opponents movement on a return)*
	5 =	distracted

Physical Feelings	1 =	excited
	2 =	energized
	3 =	unaware
	4 =	relaxed
	5 =	loose

Circle the number that matches what you felt during the competition

Competition #1	Performance Rank _____	
Emotional Control	**Mental Focus**	**Physical Feelings**
1	1	1
2	2	2
3	3	3
4	4	4
5	5	5
Notes:		

Used with Permission from the Coaching Association of Canada

Notes:

Ideal Performance State

 60

After your Second Competition

Rank your performance on the competition #2 Form
- 1 is high
- 5 is poor

Use key words as a guide to put a number value on your emotional/mental control

Emotional Control	1 =	anxious
	2 =	butterflies
	3 =	calm
	4 =	composed
	5 =	confident

Mental Focus	1 =	focused
	2 =	narrowing *(ie. focusing on the shuttle only)*
	3 =	scanning
	4 =	broadening *(ie. focusing on the opponents movement on a return)*
	5 =	distracted

Physical Feelings	1 =	excited
	2 =	energized
	3 =	unaware
	4 =	relaxed
	5 =	loose

Circle the number that matches what you felt during the competition

Competition #2	Performance Rank _____	
Emotional Control	**Mental Focus**	**Physical Feelings**
1	1	1
2	2	2
3	3	3
4	4	4
5	5	5
Notes:		

Notes:

Ideal Performance State

After your Third Competition

Rank your performance on the competition #3 Form
- 1 is high
- 5 is poor

Use key words as a guide to put a number value on your emotional/mental control

Emotional Control 1 = anxious
                   2 = butterflies
                   3 = calm
                   4 = composed
                   5 = confident

Mental Focus   1 = focused
                   2 = narrowing *(ie. focusing on the shuttle only)*
                   3 = scanning
                   4 = broadening *(ie. focusing on the opponents movement on a return)*
                   5 = distracted

Physical Feelings 1 = excited
                   2 = energized
                   3 = unaware
                   4 = relaxed
                   5 = loose

Circle the number that matches what you felt during the competition

Competition #3 Performance Rank _____		
Emotional Control	**Mental Focus**	**Physical Feelings**
1	1	1
2	2	2
3	3	3
4	4	4
5	5	5
Notes:		

Used with Permission from the Coaching Association of Canada

Notes:

Ideal Performance State

After your Fourth Competition

Rank your performance on the competition #4 Form
  - 1 is high
  - 5 is poor

Use key words as a guide to put a number value on your emotional/mental control

Emotional Control 1 = anxious
                   2 = butterflies
                   3 = calm
                   4 = composed
                   5 = confident

Mental Focus   1 = focused
                   2 = narrowing *(ie. focusing on the shuttle only)*
                   3 = scanning
                   4 = broadening *(ie. focusing on the opponents movement on a return)*
                   5 = distracted

Physical Feelings 1 = excited
                   2 = energized
                   3 = unaware
                   4 = relaxed
                   5 = loose

Circle the number that matches what you felt during the competition

Competition #5	Performance Rank _____	
Emotional Control	**Mental Focus**	**Physical Feelings**
1	1	1
2	2	2
3	3	3
4	4	4
5	5	5
Notes:		

Notes:

Ideal Performance State

 63

After your Fifth Competition

Rank your performance on the competition #5 Form
- 1 is high
- 5 is poor

Use key words as a guide to put a number value on your emotional/mental control

Emotional Control   1 =   anxious
  2 =   butterflies
  3 =   calm
  4 =   composed
  5 =   confident

Mental Focus   1 =   focused
  2 =   narrowing *(ie. focusing on the shuttle only)*
  3 =   scanning
  4 =   broadening *(ie. focusing on the opponents movement on a return)*
  5 =   distracted

Physical Feelings   1 =   excited
  2 =   energized
  3 =   unaware
  4 =   relaxed
  5 =   loose

Circle the number that matches what you felt during the competition

Competition #5 Performance Rank _____		
Emotional Control	**Mental Focus**	**Physical Feelings**
1	1	1
2	2	2
3	3	3
4	4	4
5	5	5
Notes:		

Notes:

Calculating Your I.P.S.

Using all of your information from your five competitions

1. calculate the average value selected for emotional control, mental focus and physical feelings for each competition that is ranked 1 or 2 for performance
2. record the performance rank for the best performances (ranked 1 or 2)
4. Calculate the average value for each component

This graph is your Ideal Performance State profile. Circle the word that corresponds with the best performance emotional control, mental focus and physical feelings.

Competition	1	2	3	4	5	Average
Performance Rank						
Emotional Control						
Mental Focus						
Physical Feelings						

Emotional Control	**Mental Focus**	**Physical Feelings**
1 = anxious	1 = focused	1 = excited
2 = butterflies	2 = narrowing	2 = energized
3 = calm	3 = scanning	3 = unaware
4 = composed	4 = broadening	4 = relaxed
5 = confident	5 = distracted	5 = loose

Cue Words

Now write some cue words that will help you to get to the state that will help you to perform best for each section.

Emotional Control

_____

_____

Mental Focus

_____

_____

Physical Feeling

_____

_____

Notes:

Pre-Competition Planning

How can you plan the following activities on game days that will help you perform the way you want to. Write down comments and ideas for each.:

Getting up *(ie. doing five minutes of visualization)*.

_____

Eating *(ie. eating healthy food that is not going to weigh you down)*.

_____

Making sure you have everything you need and that you know the schedule *(ie. doing a checklist)*.

_____

Washroom breaks when you get to the competition site *(ie. going before your game)*.

_____

Warming up *(ie. practicing concentration and focusing / re-focusing)*.

_____

Getting away from opponents and visitors *(ie. doing relaxation / breathing exercises)*.

_____

Mentally rehearsing and re-focusing *(ie. rehearsing game specifics in your mind)*.

_____

Using positive self-talk and monitoring your ideal performance state *(ie. using self-talk before the game starts)*.

_____

Notes:

Planning your I.P.S.

How do you get ready for competitions *(ie. check pre-competition plans, rest, etc)*?

_____

_____

_____

Write down things that you can do and words that you can say to achieve your IPS. *(ie. positive self-talk, exercises).*

_____

_____

_____

Write down some common situations that affect your ideal performance state and plan how you can respond to keep you at the level that you want *(ie. you are going to be late for the game - call a teammate or the coach and let them know).*

_____

_____

_____

Write down some common errors that you make and what kind of preparation you can do to help you focus on the correct execution *(ie. you are focused on a specific aspect of the play only - ie: use your broad focus to focus on the entire play).*

_____

_____

_____

Write down how you can be effected by your surroundings and what you can do to keep your focus on your pre-competition preparation *(ie. friends watching - use concentration skills such as picking a spot on the surface and focusing on it and away from the distraction).*

_____

_____

_____

Notes:

Pre-Competition Planning

Write down what you are going to do before the game to prepare yourself mentally and physically for the competition.

Activity

2 hours before

1.5 hours before

1 hours before

.5 hours before

Notes:

Tournament/Event Planning

Write down what you are going to do before a <u>local</u> upcoming tournament / competition to prepare yourself mentally and physically.

	Activity
1 day before	
Morning of Competition	
At the Competition site	
Before Competition	

Notes:

Tournament/Event Planning

Write down what you are going to do before an <u>out of town</u> upcoming tournament / competition to prepare yourself mentally and physically.

Activity

1 day before leaving	
1 hr before leaving	
When you get to the hotel	
Morning of First Competition	

Notes:

Main Competition Planning

Write down how you are going to use the psychological skills you have learned for badminton to help you to perform in your main competition, and in what situations you will use them .

Skill	Situation to use it in

Notes:

Life in General Planning

71

Write down how you are going to use the psychological skills you have learned for badminton to help you in every day life and in what situations you will use them.

Skill	Situation to use it in
Self-talk	use it for work or school

Notes:

Daily Organization

Use the following pages to organize your days as far as what you are going to do during the season and off season to improve the Mental, Technical and Physical skills of your competition.

Use your goal setting performance plan to organize your objectives

Example:

Day _____ Month _____ Date _____	Psychological Objective: _____ ☐
Game Day ☐ Opponents _____ *Game Goal:* _____	Technical Objective: _____ ☐ Physical Objective: _____ ☐
Practice Day ☐ Location: _____ *Practice Goal:* _____	**Nutritional Notes** _____ _____
Tournament ☐ Location: _____ *Tournament Goals:* _____	**Reflections** _____
Training Accomplishments _____ _____ _____	_____ _____

Check off the boxes of the objectives that you accomplished.

Day _____ Month _____ Date _____

Game Day ☐ Opponents _____
Game Goal:

_____

Practice Day ☐ Location: _____
Practice Goal:

_____

Tournament ☐ Location: _____
Tournament Goals:

_____

Training Accomplishments

_____

_____

_____

_____

Psychological Objective: ☐
_____

Technical Objective: ☐
_____

Physical Objective: ☐
_____

Nutritional Notes

_____

_____

Reflections

_____

_____

_____

_____

Day _____ Month _____ Date _____

Game Day ☐ Opponents _____
Game Goal:

_____

Practice Day ☐ Location: _____
Practice Goal:

_____

Tournament ☐ Location: _____
Tournament Goals:

_____

Training Accomplishments

_____

_____

_____

_____

Psychological Objective: ☐
_____

Technical Objective: ☐
_____

Physical Objective: ☐
_____

Nutritional Notes

_____

_____

Reflections

_____

_____

_____

_____

_____

Day _____ Month _____ Date _____

Game Day ☐ Opponents _____
Game Goal:

_____

Practice Day ☐ Location: _____
Practice Goal:

_____

Tournament ☐ Location: _____
Tournament Goals:

_____

Training Accomplishments

_____
_____
_____
_____
_____

Psychological Objective:
_____ ☐

Technical Objective:
_____ ☐

Physical Objective:
_____ ☐

Nutritional Notes

_____
_____

Reflections

_____
_____
_____
_____
_____

Day _____ Month _____ Date _____

Game Day ☐ Opponents _____
Game Goal:

_____

Practice Day ☐ Location: _____
Practice Goal:

_____

Tournament ☐ Location: _____
Tournament Goals:

_____

Training Accomplishments

_____
_____
_____
_____
_____

Psychological Objective:
_____ ☐

Technical Objective:
_____ ☐

Physical Objective:
_____ ☐

Nutritional Notes

_____
_____

Reflections

_____
_____
_____
_____
_____

Day _____ Month _____ Date _____

Game Day ☐ Opponents _____
Game Goal:

_____

Practice Day ☐ Location: _____
Practice Goal:

_____

Tournament ☐ Location: _____
Tournament Goals:

_____

Training Accomplishments

_____
_____
_____
_____
_____

Psychological Objective: ☐

Technical Objective: ☐

Physical Objective: ☐

Nutritional Notes

_____
_____

Reflections

_____
_____
_____
_____
_____

Day _____ Month _____ Date _____

Game Day ☐ Opponents _____
Game Goal:

_____

Practice Day ☐ Location: _____
Practice Goal:

_____

Tournament ☐ Location: _____
Tournament Goals:

_____

Training Accomplishments

_____
_____
_____
_____
_____

Psychological Objective: ☐

Technical Objective: ☐

Physical Objective: ☐

Nutritional Notes

_____
_____

Reflections

_____
_____
_____
_____
_____

Day _____ Month _____ Date _____

Game Day ☐ Opponents _____
Game Goal:
_____

Practice Day ☐ Location: _____
Practice Goal:
_____

Tournament ☐ Location: _____
Tournament Goals:
_____

Training Accomplishments

_____
_____
_____
_____
_____

Psychological Objective: ☐
_____

Technical Objective: ☐
_____

Physical Objective: ☐
_____

Nutritional Notes

_____
_____

Reflections

_____
_____
_____
_____
_____

Day _____ Month _____ Date _____

Game Day ☐ Opponents _____
Game Goal:
_____

Practice Day ☐ Location: _____
Practice Goal:
_____

Tournament ☐ Location: _____
Tournament Goals:
_____

Training Accomplishments

_____
_____
_____
_____
_____

Psychological Objective: ☐
_____

Technical Objective: ☐
_____

Physical Objective: ☐
_____

Nutritional Notes

_____
_____

Reflections

_____
_____
_____
_____
_____

Beginning Mental Training Skills for Badminton

Day ____ Month _____ Date ____

Game Day ☐ Opponents _____
Game Goal:
_____

Practice Day ☐ Location: _____
Practice Goal:
_____

Tournament ☐ Location: _____
Tournament Goals:
_____

Training Accomplishments

_____
_____
_____
_____

Psychological Objective:
_____ ☐

Technical Objective:
_____ ☐

Physical Objective:
_____ ☐

Nutritional Notes

_____
_____

Reflections

_____
_____
_____
_____

Day ____ Month _____ Date ____

Game Day ☐ Opponents _____
Game Goal:
_____

Practice Day ☐ Location: _____
Practice Goal:
_____

Tournament ☐ Location: _____
Tournament Goals:
_____

Training Accomplishments

_____
_____
_____
_____

Psychological Objective:
_____ ☐

Technical Objective:
_____ ☐

Physical Objective:
_____ ☐

Nutritional Notes

_____
_____

Reflections

_____
_____
_____
_____

Day _____ Month _____ Date _____

Game Day ☐ Opponents _____
Game Goal:

_____

Practice Day ☐ Location: _____
Practice Goal:

_____

Tournament ☐ Location: _____
Tournament Goals:

_____

Training Accomplishments

_____

_____

_____

_____

Psychological Objective: ☐

_____

Technical Objective: ☐

_____

Physical Objective: ☐

_____

Nutritional Notes

_____

_____

Reflections

_____

_____

_____

_____

_____

Day _____ Month _____ Date _____

Game Day ☐ Opponents _____
Game Goal:

_____

Practice Day ☐ Location: _____
Practice Goal:

_____

Tournament ☐ Location: _____
Tournament Goals:

_____

Training Accomplishments

_____

_____

_____

_____

Psychological Objective: ☐

_____

Technical Objective: ☐

_____

Physical Objective: ☐

_____

Nutritional Notes

_____

_____

Reflections

_____

_____

_____

_____

Day _____ Month _____ Date _____

Game Day ☐ Opponents _____
Game Goal:

_____

Practice Day ☐ Location: _____
Practice Goal:

_____

Tournament ☐ Location: _____
Tournament Goals:

_____

Training Accomplishments

_____
_____
_____
_____

Psychological Objective:
_____ ☐

Technical Objective:
_____ ☐

Physical Objective:
_____ ☐

Nutritional Notes

_____
_____

Reflections

_____
_____
_____

Day _____ Month _____ Date _____

Game Day ☐ Opponents _____
Game Goal:

_____

Practice Day ☐ Location: _____
Practice Goal:

_____

Tournament ☐ Location: _____
Tournament Goals:

_____

Training Accomplishments

_____
_____
_____

Psychological Objective:
_____ ☐

Technical Objective:
_____ ☐

Physical Objective:
_____ ☐

Nutritional Notes

_____
_____

Reflections

_____
_____
_____

Day _____ Month _____ Date _____

Psychological Objective:

☐

Game Day ☐ Opponents _____

Technical Objective:

☐

Game Goal:

Physical Objective:

☐

_____

Practice Day ☐ Location: _____

Nutritional Notes

Practice Goal:

_____

_____

Tournament ☐ Location: _____

Reflections

Tournament Goals:

_____

_____

Training Accomplishments

_____

_____

_____

_____

_____

_____

_____

_____

_____

Day _____ Month _____ Date _____

Psychological Objective:

☐

Game Day ☐ Opponents _____

Technical Objective:

☐

Game Goal:

Physical Objective:

☐

_____

Practice Day ☐ Location: _____

Nutritional Notes

Practice Goal:

_____

_____

Tournament ☐ Location: _____

Reflections

Tournament Goals:

_____

_____

Training Accomplishments

_____

_____

_____

_____

_____

_____

_____

_____

_____

Day _____ Month _____ Date _____

Game Day ☐ Opponents _____
Game Goal:

_____

Practice Day ☐ Location: _____
Practice Goal:

_____

Tournament ☐ Location: _____
Tournament Goals:

_____

Training Accomplishments

_____
_____
_____
_____

Psychological Objective: ☐

Technical Objective: ☐

Physical Objective: ☐

Nutritional Notes

_____
_____

Reflections

_____
_____
_____
_____

Day _____ Month _____ Date _____

Game Day ☐ Opponents _____
Game Goal:

_____

Practice Day ☐ Location: _____
Practice Goal:

_____

Tournament ☐ Location: _____
Tournament Goals:

_____

Training Accomplishments

_____
_____
_____
_____

Psychological Objective: ☐

Technical Objective: ☐

Physical Objective: ☐

Nutritional Notes

_____
_____

Reflections

_____
_____
_____
_____

Day _____ Month _____ Date _____

Game Day ☐ Opponents _____
Game Goal:
_____

Practice Day ☐ Location: _____
Practice Goal:
_____

Tournament ☐ Location: _____
Tournament Goals:
_____

Training Accomplishments
_____
_____
_____
_____

Psychological Objective: ☐
_____

Technical Objective: ☐
_____

Physical Objective: ☐
_____

Nutritional Notes
_____
_____

Reflections
_____
_____
_____
_____
_____

Day _____ Month _____ Date _____

Game Day ☐ Opponents _____
Game Goal:
_____

Practice Day ☐ Location: _____
Practice Goal:
_____

Tournament ☐ Location: _____
Tournament Goals:
_____

Training Accomplishments
_____
_____
_____

Psychological Objective: ☐
_____

Technical Objective: ☐
_____

Physical Objective: ☐
_____

Nutritional Notes
_____
_____

Reflections
_____
_____
_____
_____

Day _____ Month _____ Date _____

Game Day ☐ Opponents _____
Game Goal:

_____

Practice Day ☐ Location: _____
Practice Goal:

_____

Tournament ☐ Location: _____
Tournament Goals:

_____

Training Accomplishments

_____

_____

_____

_____

Psychological Objective: ☐

_____

Technical Objective: ☐

_____

Physical Objective: ☐

_____

Nutritional Notes

_____

_____

Reflections

_____

_____

_____

_____

_____

Day _____ Month _____ Date _____

Game Day ☐ Opponents _____
Game Goal:

_____

Practice Day ☐ Location: _____
Practice Goal:

_____

Tournament ☐ Location: _____
Tournament Goals:

_____

Training Accomplishments

_____

_____

_____

_____

Psychological Objective: ☐

_____

Technical Objective: ☐

_____

Physical Objective: ☐

_____

Nutritional Notes

_____

_____

Reflections

_____

_____

_____

_____

_____

Day _____ Month _____ Date _____

Game Day ☐ Opponents _____
Game Goal:

_____

Practice Day ☐ Location: _____
Practice Goal:

_____

Tournament ☐ Location: _____
Tournament Goals:

_____

Training Accomplishments

_____
_____
_____
_____
_____

Psychological Objective: ☐

Technical Objective: ☐

Physical Objective: ☐

Nutritional Notes

_____
_____

Reflections

_____
_____
_____
_____
_____

Day _____ Month _____ Date _____

Game Day ☐ Opponents _____
Game Goal:

_____

Practice Day ☐ Location: _____
Practice Goal:

_____

Tournament ☐ Location: _____
Tournament Goals:

_____

Training Accomplishments

_____
_____
_____

Psychological Objective: ☐

Technical Objective: ☐

Physical Objective: ☐

Nutritional Notes

_____

Reflections

_____
_____
_____
_____

Day _____ Month _____ Date _____

Game Day ☐ Opponents _____
Game Goal:

_____

Practice Day ☐ Location: _____
Practice Goal:

_____

Tournament ☐ Location: _____
Tournament Goals:

_____

Training Accomplishments

_____
_____
_____
_____
_____

Psychological Objective:
_____ ☐

Technical Objective:
_____ ☐

Physical Objective:
_____ ☐

Nutritional Notes

_____
_____

Reflections

_____
_____
_____
_____
_____

Day _____ Month _____ Date _____

Game Day ☐ Opponents _____
Game Goal:

_____

Practice Day ☐ Location: _____
Practice Goal:

_____

Tournament ☐ Location: _____
Tournament Goals:

_____

Training Accomplishments

_____
_____
_____
_____

Psychological Objective:
_____ ☐

Technical Objective:
_____ ☐

Physical Objective:
_____ ☐

Nutritional Notes

_____
_____

Reflections

_____
_____
_____
_____
_____

Day _____ Month _____ Date _____

Game Day ☐ Opponents _____
Game Goal:
_____

Practice Day ☐ Location: _____
Practice Goal:
_____

Tournament ☐ Location: _____
Tournament Goals:
_____

Training Accomplishments

_____
_____
_____
_____
_____

Psychological Objective: ☐
_____

Technical Objective: ☐
_____

Physical Objective: ☐
_____

Nutritional Notes

_____
_____

Reflections

_____
_____
_____
_____

Day _____ Month _____ Date _____

Game Day ☐ Opponents _____
Game Goal:
_____

Practice Day ☐ Location: _____
Practice Goal:
_____

Tournament ☐ Location: _____
Tournament Goals:
_____

Training Accomplishments

_____
_____
_____
_____
_____

Psychological Objective: ☐
_____

Technical Objective: ☐
_____

Physical Objective: ☐
_____

Nutritional Notes

_____
_____

Reflections

_____
_____
_____
_____

Day _____ Month _____ Date _____

Game Day ☐ Opponents _____
Game Goal:

_____

Practice Day ☐ Location: _____
Practice Goal:

_____

Tournament ☐ Location: _____
Tournament Goals:

_____

Training Accomplishments

_____
_____
_____
_____

Psychological Objective:
_____ ☐

Technical Objective:
_____ ☐

Physical Objective:
_____ ☐

Nutritional Notes

_____

Reflections

_____
_____
_____
_____

Day _____ Month _____ Date _____

Game Day ☐ Opponents _____
Game Goal:

_____

Practice Day ☐ Location: _____
Practice Goal:

_____

Tournament ☐ Location: _____
Tournament Goals:

_____

Training Accomplishments

_____
_____
_____
_____

Psychological Objective:
_____ ☐

Technical Objective:
_____ ☐

Physical Objective:
_____ ☐

Nutritional Notes

_____

Reflections

_____
_____
_____
_____

Day _____ Month _____ Date _____

Game Day ☐ Opponents _____
Game Goal:

_____

Practice Day ☐ Location: _____
Practice Goal:

_____

Tournament ☐ Location: _____
Tournament Goals:

_____

Training Accomplishments

_____

_____

_____

_____

Psychological Objective: ☐

Technical Objective: ☐

Physical Objective: ☐

Nutritional Notes

_____

_____

Reflections

_____

_____

_____

_____

_____

Day _____ Month _____ Date _____

Game Day ☐ Opponents _____
Game Goal:

_____

Practice Day ☐ Location: _____
Practice Goal:

_____

Tournament ☐ Location: _____
Tournament Goals:

_____

Training Accomplishments

_____

_____

_____

_____

Psychological Objective: ☐

Technical Objective: ☐

Physical Objective: ☐

Nutritional Notes

_____

_____

Reflections

_____

_____

_____

_____

_____

Day _____ Month _____ Date _____

Game Day ☐ Opponents _____
Game Goal:

_____

Practice Day ☐ Location: _____
Practice Goal:

_____

Tournament ☐ Location: _____
Tournament Goals:

_____

Training Accomplishments

_____
_____
_____
_____

Psychological Objective:

_____ ☐

Technical Objective:

_____ ☐

Physical Objective:

_____ ☐

Nutritional Notes

_____
_____

Reflections

_____
_____
_____
_____

Day _____ Month _____ Date _____

Game Day ☐ Opponents _____
Game Goal:

_____

Practice Day ☐ Location: _____
Practice Goal:

_____

Tournament ☐ Location: _____
Tournament Goals:

_____

Training Accomplishments

_____
_____
_____
_____

Psychological Objective:

_____ ☐

Technical Objective:

_____ ☐

Physical Objective:

_____ ☐

Nutritional Notes

_____
_____

Reflections

_____
_____
_____
_____

Day _____ **Month** _____ **Date** _____

Game Day ☐ Opponents _____
Game Goal:

_____

Practice Day ☐ Location: _____
Practice Goal:

_____

Tournament ☐ Location: _____
Tournament Goals:

_____

Training Accomplishments

_____
_____
_____
_____
_____

Psychological Objective:
_____ ☐

Technical Objective:
_____ ☐

Physical Objective:
_____ ☐

Nutritional Notes

_____
_____

Reflections

_____
_____
_____
_____
_____
_____

Day _____ **Month** _____ **Date** _____

Game Day ☐ Opponents _____
Game Goal:

_____

Practice Day ☐ Location: _____
Practice Goal:

_____

Tournament ☐ Location: _____
Tournament Goals:

_____

Training Accomplishments

_____
_____
_____
_____
_____

Psychological Objective:
_____ ☐

Technical Objective:
_____ ☐

Physical Objective:
_____ ☐

Nutritional Notes

_____
_____

Reflections

_____
_____
_____
_____
_____
_____

Day _____ Month _____ Date _____

Psychological Objective:
_____ ☐

Technical Objective:
_____ ☐

Physical Objective:
_____ ☐

Game Day ☐ Opponents _____
Game Goal:

_____

Practice Day ☐ Location: _____
Practice Goal:

_____

Tournament ☐ Location: _____
Tournament Goals:

_____

Nutritional Notes

_____

_____

Reflections

_____

Training Accomplishments

_____

_____

_____

_____

_____

_____

_____

_____

_____

Day _____ Month _____ Date _____

Psychological Objective:
_____ ☐

Technical Objective:
_____ ☐

Physical Objective:
_____ ☐

Game Day ☐ Opponents _____
Game Goal:

_____

Practice Day ☐ Location: _____
Practice Goal:

_____

Tournament ☐ Location: _____
Tournament Goals:

_____

Nutritional Notes

_____

_____

Reflections

_____

Training Accomplishments

_____

_____

_____

_____

_____

_____

_____

Day _____ Month _____ Date _____

Psychological Objective: _____ ☐

Technical Objective: _____ ☐

Physical Objective: _____ ☐

Game Day ☐ Opponents _____

Game Goal:

_____

Practice Day ☐ Location: _____

Practice Goal:

_____

Tournament ☐ Location: _____

Tournament Goals:

_____

Nutritional Notes

_____

_____

Reflections

Training Accomplishments

_____

_____

_____

_____

_____

_____

_____

_____

_____

Day _____ Month _____ Date _____

Psychological Objective: _____ ☐

Technical Objective: _____ ☐

Physical Objective: _____ ☐

Game Day ☐ Opponents _____

Game Goal:

_____

Practice Day ☐ Location: _____

Practice Goal:

_____

Tournament ☐ Location: _____

Tournament Goals:

_____

Nutritional Notes

_____

_____

Reflections

Training Accomplishments

_____

_____

_____

_____

_____

_____

_____

_____

_____

Day _____ Month _____ Date _____

Game Day ☐ Opponents _____
Game Goal:
_____

Practice Day ☐ Location: _____
Practice Goal:
_____

Tournament ☐ Location: _____
Tournament Goals:
_____

Training Accomplishments

_____
_____
_____
_____
_____

Psychological Objective: ☐
_____

Technical Objective: ☐
_____

Physical Objective: ☐
_____

Nutritional Notes

_____
_____

Reflections

_____
_____
_____
_____

Day _____ Month _____ Date _____

Game Day ☐ Opponents _____
Game Goal:
_____

Practice Day ☐ Location: _____
Practice Goal:
_____

Tournament ☐ Location: _____
Tournament Goals:
_____

Training Accomplishments

_____
_____
_____
_____
_____

Psychological Objective: ☐
_____

Technical Objective: ☐
_____

Physical Objective: ☐
_____

Nutritional Notes

_____
_____

Reflections

_____
_____
_____
_____

Beginning Mental Training Skills for Badminton

Day _____ Month _____ Date _____

Game Day ☐ Opponents _____
Game Goal:

_____

Practice Day ☐ Location: _____
Practice Goal:

_____

Tournament ☐ Location: _____
Tournament Goals:

_____

Training Accomplishments

_____
_____
_____
_____
_____

Psychological Objective:
_____ ☐

Technical Objective:
_____ ☐

Physical Objective:
_____ ☐

Nutritional Notes

_____

Reflections

_____
_____
_____
_____
_____

Day _____ Month _____ Date _____

Game Day ☐ Opponents _____
Game Goal:

_____

Practice Day ☐ Location: _____
Practice Goal:

_____

Tournament ☐ Location: _____
Tournament Goals:

_____

Training Accomplishments

_____
_____
_____
_____
_____

Psychological Objective:
_____ ☐

Technical Objective:
_____ ☐

Physical Objective:
_____ ☐

Nutritional Notes

_____

Reflections

_____
_____
_____
_____
_____

Day _____ Month _____ Date _____

Game Day ☐ Opponents _____
Game Goal:

_____

Practice Day ☐ Location: _____
Practice Goal:

_____

Tournament ☐ Location: _____
Tournament Goals:

_____

Training Accomplishments

_____

_____

_____

_____

Psychological Objective:
_____ ☐

Technical Objective:
_____ ☐

Physical Objective:
_____ ☐

Nutritional Notes

_____

_____

Reflections

_____

_____

_____

_____

Day _____ Month _____ Date _____

Game Day ☐ Opponents _____
Game Goal:

_____

Practice Day ☐ Location: _____
Practice Goal:

_____

Tournament ☐ Location: _____
Tournament Goals:

_____

Training Accomplishments

_____

_____

_____

_____

Psychological Objective:
_____ ☐

Technical Objective:
_____ ☐

Physical Objective:
_____ ☐

Nutritional Notes

_____

_____

Reflections

_____

_____

_____

Day _____ Month _____ Date _____

Game Day ☐ Opponents _____
Game Goal:

_____

Practice Day ☐ Location: _____
Practice Goal:

_____

Tournament ☐ Location: _____
Tournament Goals:

_____

Training Accomplishments

_____
_____
_____
_____
_____

Psychological Objective: ☐

_____

Technical Objective: ☐

_____

Physical Objective: ☐

_____

Nutritional Notes

_____
_____

Reflections

_____
_____
_____
_____
_____

Day _____ Month _____ Date _____

Game Day ☐ Opponents _____
Game Goal:

_____

Practice Day ☐ Location: _____
Practice Goal:

_____

Tournament ☐ Location: _____
Tournament Goals:

_____

Training Accomplishments

_____
_____
_____
_____
_____

Psychological Objective: ☐

_____

Technical Objective: ☐

_____

Physical Objective: ☐

Nutritional Notes

_____
_____

Reflections

_____
_____
_____
_____
_____

Day _____ Month _____ Date _____

Game Day ☐ Opponents _____
Game Goal:

_____

Practice Day ☐ Location: _____
Practice Goal:

_____

Tournament ☐ Location: _____
Tournament Goals:

_____

Training Accomplishments

_____
_____
_____
_____
_____

Psychological Objective: ☐

_____

Technical Objective: ☐

_____

Physical Objective: ☐

_____

Nutritional Notes

_____
_____

Reflections

_____
_____
_____
_____

Day _____ Month _____ Date _____

Game Day ☐ Opponents _____
Game Goal:

_____

Practice Day ☐ Location: _____
Practice Goal:

_____

Tournament ☐ Location: _____
Tournament Goals:

_____

Training Accomplishments

_____
_____
_____
_____
_____

Psychological Objective: ☐

_____

Technical Objective: ☐

_____

Physical Objective: ☐

_____

Nutritional Notes

_____
_____

Reflections

_____
_____
_____
_____

Day _____ Month _____ Date _____

Psychological Objective:

☐

Technical Objective:

☐

Physical Objective:

☐

Game Day ☐ Opponents _____
Game Goal:

Practice Day ☐ Location: _____
Practice Goal:

Tournament ☐ Location: _____
Tournament Goals:

Nutritional Notes

Reflections

Training Accomplishments

Day _____ Month _____ Date _____

Psychological Objective:

☐

Technical Objective:

☐

Physical Objective:

☐

Game Day ☐ Opponents _____
Game Goal:

Practice Day ☐ Location: _____
Practice Goal:

Tournament ☐ Location: _____
Tournament Goals:

Nutritional Notes

Reflections

Training Accomplishments

Day _____ Month _____ Date _____

Psychological Objective:
_____ ☐

Technical Objective:
_____ ☐

Physical Objective:
_____ ☐

Game Day ☐ Opponents _____
Game Goal:

_____

Practice Day ☐ Location: _____
Practice Goal:

_____

Tournament ☐ Location: _____
Tournament Goals:

_____

Nutritional Notes

_____
_____

Reflections

Training Accomplishments

_____
_____
_____
_____

_____
_____
_____
_____

Day _____ Month _____ Date _____

Psychological Objective:
_____ ☐

Technical Objective:
_____ ☐

Physical Objective:
_____ ☐

Game Day ☐ Opponents _____
Game Goal:

_____

Practice Day ☐ Location: _____
Practice Goal:

_____

Tournament ☐ Location: _____
Tournament Goals:

_____

Nutritional Notes

_____
_____

Reflections

Training Accomplishments

_____
_____
_____

_____
_____
_____
_____

Journal

Use the following pages to record how your progress is going during the pre-season, season and off season.

Remember to record the date so you can refer back to it if you wish to see how your progress is going. Also record any special situations or circumstances that may have affected your feelings.

Are you finding the season difficult?

Are things coming to you easier as the season goes on?

How is your season going in general?

Are you getting along with your teammates?

Write anything you want, for whatever reason, it is your journal.

Beginning Mental Training Skills for Badminton

Date	Reflections

Beginning Mental Training Skills for Badminton

Date	Reflections

Beginning Mental Training Skills for Badminton

Date	Reflections

Beginning Mental Training Skills for Badminton

Date	Reflections

Beginning Mental Training Skills for Badminton

Date	Reflections

Beginning Mental Training Skills for Badminton

Date	Reflections

Beginning Mental Training Skills for Badminton

Date	Reflections

Beginning Mental Training Skills for Badminton

Date	Reflections

Beginning Mental Training Skills for Badminton

Date	Reflections

Beginning Mental Training Skills for Badminton

Date	Reflections

Beginning Mental Training Skills for Badminton

Date	Reflections

Beginning Mental Training Skills for Badminton

Date	Reflections

Beginning Mental Training Skills for Badminton

Date	Reflections

Beginning Mental Training Skills for Badminton

Date	Reflections

Beginning Mental Training Skills for Badminton

Date	Reflections

Enjoy the Process!!

Printed in Great Britain
by Amazon

53272886R00110